THE AUSTRALIAN ARCHAEOLOGIST'S
BOOK OF QUOTATIONS

THE AUSTRALIAN ARCHAEOLOGIST'S BOOK OF QUOTATIONS

EDITED BY MIKE SMITH AND BILLY GRIFFITHS

MONASH University Publishing

Monash University Publishing
Matheson Library and Information Services Building
40 Exhibition Walk, Monash University
Clayton, Victoria 3800, Australia
www.publishing.monash.edu

Monash University Publishing brings to the world publications which advance the best traditions of humane and enlightened thought. Monash University Publishing titles pass through a rigorous process of independent peer review.
www.publishing.monash.edu/books/aabq-9781922235749.html

Series: Australian History
Design: Les Thomas
Photos courtesy of Mike Smith (Chapters 1, 5, 6, 7 and 8), Billy Griffiths (Chapters 3 and 4) and Darrell Lewis (Chapter 2).

Cover image: Excavations at Malakunanja II (Madjedbebe), western Arnhem Land, 1989. The excavators argued this sequence showed Australia was first colonised 50-60,000 years ago. This quickly entered the public domain and '50,000 years' began to frame popular perceptions of the antiquity of Aboriginal Australia. © M Smith.

National Library of Australia Cataloguing-in-Publication entry:

Creator:	Smith, M. A. (Michael Alexander), 1955- author.
Title:	The Australian Archaeologist's Book of Quotations / Mike Smith and Billy Griffiths.
ISBN:	9781922235749 (paperback)
Series:	Australian History (Monash University Publishing)
Notes:	Includes index.
Subjects:	Archaeology--Australia--Quotations, maxims, etc.
	Archaeology--Australia--Miscellanea.
	Aboriginal Australians--History.
	Aboriginal Australians--Antiquities.
	Aboriginal Australians--Land tenure--History
Other Creators:	Griffiths, Billy, author.
Dewey Number:	930.102

Printed in Australia by Griffin Press an Accredited ISO AS/NZS 14001:2004 Environmental Management System printer.

CONTENTS

PREFACE

WHEN I AM writing a popular piece – or speaking to a general audience – I find myself reaching for that memorable, but only half-remembered quote or phrase, that somehow captures what I want to say. One of the purposes of a book of quotations like this is to help you easily find those pithy apposite quotes – and their source. And like me, you may well find that the actual words are subtly different to the version you remembered. But of course this is not the only role of a book of quotations. It is also a guide to the catch phrases of a discipline. It provides a snapshot of the history and concerns of archaeology – in a sense a 'map' of the field. Above all, a book like this encourages an appreciation of good writing and a well-turned phrase.

The only comparable book of quotations for the field is *The Archaeologist's Book of Quotations* by K. Kris Hirst (Left Coast Press, 2010). But, perhaps inevitably, this has no coverage of Australia. None at all. So here we have tried to address this.

The majority of quotations here are by Australian researchers or deal with the Australian context. Others are included simply because we find them useful and pertinent in our own work. It would be impossible to leave out those pithy phrases from Mortimer Wheeler or Kent Flannery (though few students seem to know them today). So in some ways, this is a book of quotations *for* Australian archaeologists not simply *by* them. All of the quotations here have been chosen because they are succinct or catchy summations of an issue. We have extended beyond archaeology and archaeological practice to include sections on Aboriginal society, climate and landscape change, fire and the desert, because these are areas of special relevance to Australian researchers. We have avoided quotes that are self-consciously 'clever', that smack too much of artifice, or that were written specifically with an eye to notoriety.

I see this little book as part of the 'cultural paraphernalia' of Australian archaeology: a mature discipline inevitably has its dictionaries, histories, encyclopaedias and popular works – and now a 'book of quotations'. These are not the main aims of a field, but they help increase its accessibility.

It is important to stress that inclusion of a passage does not mean the editors agree with its sentiments. Some – such as J.P. Droop's comments in 1915 on 'mixed-gender' digs or R.J.C. Atkinson's views in 1946 on preferring paid 'navvies' rather than 'unskilled amateurs' for archaeological work – no longer reflect archaeological practice. Others – with their repeated references to 'men', 'man' and 'his' – are definitely a bit dated. And others – such as the famous passage from Spencer and Gillen (1927) about Australia being the 'home and refuge of creatures, often crude and quaint' – should be seen as products of their time. They are included in this collection because one of the roles of a book of quotations is to encourage a critical analysis and review of the field. Modern archaeological research in Australia, New Guinea and the Pacific region began as a reaction to such evolutionary views, taking the position that the peoples of the region had their own histories which could be recovered using archaeological field techniques.

The quotations are arranged in eight broad sections and numbered sequentially within each. The index provides a guide arranged by author and by the key phrase. We are grateful to all those who gave us permission to include their words, including the poetry of Mark O'Connor. The photographs in this book are courtesy of the editors and Darrell Lewis.

Mike Smith, July 2015

AUSTRALIAN ARCHAEOLOGY has been involved in a great enterprise over the last sixty years, uncovering the deep past of a desert continent and the history of its first people. This book helps map the development of the field and gives us a snapshot of the people, the places, and the ideas that have driven the recent revolution of Australia's timescale. It is also a meditation on science and place, culture and politics, deep time and the Dreaming. Woven in amongst these quotations is the story of how, as a nation, we are coming to terms with ancient Australia.

A book of quotations naturally reflects the passions and idiosyncrasies of the compilers. The subjects addressed here are diverse. The entries have been drawn from letters and journals, histories and poems, newspapers and novels. Some are included because they contain an oft-used catch phrase or a critical insight into ancient Australia. Other entries have been rescued from relative obscurity and are presented here to surprise, inform and delight readers. And occasionally we have included a brief anecdote or description, because we believe there is a story to be told here, as well as a reference book to be compiled.

We do not presume this to be the definitive guide to all that has been said and done by Australian archaeologists and about Australian archaeology. Instead, we hope this book will open conversations about the field and inspire reflection and review. Inevitably, we have missed worthy quotations in this selection – and we encourage readers to make their own additions. Our consolation is that this book might become the subject of discussion and create new opportunities for such quotations to be brought to light.

We regret that there are many who have played a significant role in the development of the field whose words are not included in this collection. It must be emphasised that the exclusion, or degree of representation, of particular writers is no reflection of their perceived value or contribution to the history and culture of Australian archaeology. It may simply reflect the dialectic between scholarship and writing: not everyone writes in epigrams, and quality is not the same as quotability.

Archaeology, as a discipline, straddles the border between the arts and the sciences. This book, compiled by a desert archaeologist and a historian, aims to move freely across that border and encourage a dialogue between the sciences and humanities.

Billy Griffiths, July 2015

1: ON AUSTRALIAN PREHISTORY

A series of quotations that map Australian prehistory, showing early pre-occupation with evolutionary perspectives followed by a more nuanced concern with the nitty-gritty of the archaeological record.

ANON
Graffiti

(1-1) 40,000 Years is a Long, Long Time
40,000 Years Still on My Mind

Graffiti on Redfern station, Sydney, 2013.

ANDREW ARTHUR ABBIE
On the origin of the Tasmanians

(1-2) The evidence available thus supports the idea that the Tasmanians owed their origin to the chance that some drifting Melanesians were cast ashore on Tasmania.

The Original Australians (Sydney: A.H. & A.W. Reed, 1969), 229.

JIM ALLEN
On crossing Bass Strait

(1-3) That night, as we gazed northwards over Bass Strait, we knew the answer to Flinders' conundrum, although the final proof would require years more research to demonstrate. People had walked, dry-shod, to Tasmania, at a time when lowered sea levels exposed dry land, at a minimum, more than 8,000 years ago.

'Hunter Gatherers as Colonisers: The First Humans East of the Wallace Line', The Mulvaney Lecture, Australian National University, 24 March 1999.

CHARLES BARRETT
On the Devon Downs-Tartanga dig

(1-4) This is the opening chapter of the Romance of Excavation in Australia. It should stimulate research and may lead to a series of expeditions [in] the quest of prehistoric man in our country.

'Ancient Man in Australia; Relics found in rocks; Tartanga fossils will be world famous', *Herald*, 18 July 1930.

JOHN BEATON
On the archaeological exploration of Australia

(1-5) …at this time in Australian prehistory it appears that the earliest phase, the 'Captain Cook Phase' of discovery is largely over. It seemed to me that the best contribution that scholars of my generation could offer is a regional exploration that might be likened to the 'Major Mitchell Phase', where the discoveries of the primary explorers are put into regional context.

Dangerous harvest: investigations in the late prehistoric occupation of upland south-east central Queensland, PhD thesis, Australian National University, 1977, 19.

On ice age Tasmania

(1-6) One of the very challenging cultural images … is that of the people who lived in the Southern Forests while the last glaciation waxed and waned around them. The surprise is that they did it at all. Extreme climate, extremely low fat diets, extremely rugged country. Why not leave while the Bassian Bridge was intact? Perhaps some did.

'Tasmania – An extreme version of Australia', in A. Anderson and T. Murray (eds.), *Australian Archaeologist: Collected papers in honour of Jim Allen* (Canberra: Coombs Academic Publishing, ANU, 2000), 182-186, 184.

BARBARA BENDER
On social intensification

(1-7) …in ceremonial life lie the seeds of increased demands, more
food for feasting, more goods for exchange, more intensive
relations between elder and initiate, and between elder and
wives.

'Gatherer-Hunter Intensification', in A. Sheridan and G.N. Bailey
(eds.), *Economic Archaeology: towards an integration of ecological and social
approaches* (Oxford: B.A.R., 1981), 149-57, 154.

JOSEPH BIRDSELL
On the colonisation of Australia

(1-8) It is highly probable that there was a constant if somewhat
straggling trickle of small groups of human beings over all or
most of the routes.

'The recalibration of a paradigm for the first peopling of Greater
Australia', in J. Allen, J. Golson and R. Jones (eds.), *Sunda and Sahul:
Prehistoric Studies in Southeast Asia, Melanesia and Australia* (London:
Academic Press, 1977), 113-67, 123.

GEOFFREY BLAINEY
On Australian economic history

(1-9) I used to begin a course on Australian economic history in
the accepted manner with the European explorations of the
eighteenth century until one day the archaeologist, John
Mulvaney, enquired what I said about the earlier 99 per cent
of time embraced by the human history of Australia.

The Triumph of the Nomads: a history of ancient Australia (South Melbourne:
Macmillan, 1975), viii.

On the effects of the last marine transgression

(1-10) Salt water drowned perhaps one-seventh of the land…
Every tribal group on the coast 15,000 years ago must have

slowly lost its entire territory … a succession of retreats must have occurred. The slow exodus of refugees, the sorting out of peoples and the struggle for territories probably led to many wounds and deaths as well as new alliances.

The Triumph of the Nomads: a history of ancient Australia (South Melbourne: Macmillan, 1975), 89-91.

SANDRA BOWDLER
On shell middens

(1-11) It is worth remembering that a shell midden is itself a particular sort of artefact, deposited and structured by the unremitting efforts of woman the gatherer.

'Hook, line & dilly bag: an interpretation of an Australian coastal shell midden', *Mankind* 10(4) (1976), 248-258, 256.

On the coastal colonisation of Australia

(1-12) …Australia was colonised by people adapted to a coastal way of life.

'The coastal colonisation of Australia', in J. Allen, R. Jones & J. Golson (eds.), *Sunda and Sahul: Prehistoric Studies in Southeast Asia, Melanesia and Australia* (London: Academic Press, 1977), 205-246, 205

On a coastal economy in the inland

(1-13) …if we look closely at the economic evidence from the older dated Willandra sites, it can be interpreted as representing a coastal economy 'transliterated' to a freshwater situation.

'The coastal colonisation of Australia', in J. Allen, R. Jones & J. Golson (eds.), *Sunda and Sahul: Prehistoric Studies in Southeast Asia, Melanesia and Australia* (London: Academic Press, 1977), 205-246, 213.

On Bondi points

(1-14) It is hardly a coincidence that Australia's best known
    prehistoric artefact is named after its most famous beach.

'Valla madness: Australian Archaeological Association conference on
coastal prehistory in Australia', in S. Bowdler (ed.), *Coastal Archaeology
in Eastern Australia: Proceedings of the 1980 Valla Conference on Australian*
Prehistory, Occasional Papers in Prehistory 11 (Canberra: Australian
National University, 1982), v.

JIM BOWLER
On the discoveries at Lake Mungo

(1-15) The association here of complex burial ritual (Mungo
    3) involving anointing with ochre at this time presents
    one of the dramatic mysteries of ancient human cultural
    development. In death, the story of that person illuminates
    our understanding of those ancient occupants and the Ice
    Age environments that supported them.

'Willandra Lakes revisited: Environmental framework for human
occupation', *Archaeology in Oceania* 33(3), Special Issue (1998), 120-55, 120.

H.Y.L. (HENRY) BROWN
On mistaking rock engravings for fossil tracks

(1-16) On some of the hard blocks of quartzite and quartzose
    sandstone near this place there are marks somewhat
    resembling the impressions of the feet of human beings,
    kangaroo, birds, etc., which are considered to be fossil tracks.
    On examination they appear to be merely rough imitations
    of such, the smooth surface of the rock having been
    removed by some hard instrument to a slight depth, the
    pitted marks of such action being plainly visible.

'Report of Government Geologist', *South Australian Parliamentary Papers*
4(146) (1883), 1-5, 5.

DENIS BYRNE
On the meeting of cultures

(1-17) ...the conventional use of the term 'contact', though, now seem rather too hard edged, evoking as it does an image of cultures as billiard balls and a nineteenth century vision in which 'European culture bumped into non-European culture without merging'. Nicholas Thomas's term, 'entanglement', which he uses primarily in the context of cross-cultural traffic in material culture, seems preferable. It is an entanglement which occurs in the processes of exchange, borrowing, modification, and reworking which are a typical accompaniment to the meeting of cultures.

'Deep nation: Australia's acquisition of an indigenous past', *Aboriginal History* 20 (1998), 82-107, 83.

SCOTT CANE
On Malakunanja II (Madjedbebe)

(1-18) Faded paintings cast an ancestral shadow across the shelter walls, and its floor contains histories of ages past.

First Footprints: The epic story of the First Australians (Crows Nest, NSW: Allen & Unwin, 2013), 66.

VERE GORDON CHILDE
On finding Australian archaeology boring

(1-19) Australian archaeology has possibilities though I could not possibly get interested. There are varieties of stone implement types – all horribly boring unless you're a flint fan – some stratified sites, rock drawings and paintings of uncertain age.

Letter to O.G.S. Crawford, 6 August 1957, cited in R. Jones, 'Dating the human colonization of Australia: Radiocarbon and luminescence revolutions', *Proceedings of the British Academy* 99 (1998), 37-65, 39.

ANNIE CLARKE
On putative stone houses in western Victoria

(1-20) To return to the theme of the romancing of the stones there are clear examples where the archaeology has escaped into a more public realm and undergone a transformation of romantic assertion.

'Romancing the Stones: The cultural construction of an archaeological landscape in the Western District of Victoria', *Archaeology in Oceania* 29 (1994), 1-15, 13.

GRAHAME CLARK
On simple flake stone tools

(1-21) The crude and colourless nature of this industry may serve to remind us that the original Australian aborigines issued from one of the most unenterprising parts of the Late Pleistocene world.

'Australian stone age', in K. Jazdzewski (ed.), *Liber Iosepho Kostrzewski octogenario a veneratoribus dicatus* (Warsaw: Ossolineum, Polish Academy of Sciences, 1968), 17-28, 21-2.

ALFRED W. CROSBY
On a naïve ecosystem

(1-22) The Americas and Australasia have provided windfall advantages to humanity twice, once in the Paleolithic and again in the last half millennium.

Ecological Imperialism: The biological expansion of Europe, 900-1900 (Cambridge: Cambridge University Press, 1994), 307.

IAIN DAVIDSON ET AL.
On the trade in stone axes

(1-23) ...we have shown the fine grain of the archaeological record associated with the movement of axes, the subtlety of the symbolic world through which some of the materials passed, and the possibility that the trade and the symbolic construction of the world were interwoven.

I. Davidson, N. Cook, M. Fisher, M. Ridges, J. Ross and S. Sutton, 'Archaeology in another country: exchange and symbols in north-west central Queensland', in I. Macfarlane, M.J. Mountain and R. Paton (eds.), *Many Exchanges: archaeology, history, community and the work of Isabel McBryde* (Canberra: Aboriginal History Inc., 2005), 103-130, 125.

CHARLES DORTCH
On submerged archaeological sites

(1-24) Much of Australian prehistory lies under water.

'Prehistory down under: Archaeological investigations of submerged aboriginal sites at Lake Jasper, Western Australia', *Antiquity* 71(271) (1997), 116-123, 116.

ROBERT DREWE
A novelist's semi-fictionalised account of the discoveries at Lake Mungo

(1-25) …a small, pretty skull. It had been cremated and smashed into hundreds of fragments, so that each piece resembled the tannin-stained shard of a broken teacup. … She was built like a ballerina.

Grace (Camberwell, VIC: Viking, 2005), 97, 101.

TIM FLANNERY
On the colonisation of Australasia

(1-26) Freed from the ecological constraints of their homeland and armed with weapons honed in the relentless arms race of Eurasia, the colonisers of the 'new' lands were poised to become the world's first future eaters.

The Future Eaters: An ecological history of the Australasian lands and people (Sydney: Reed New Holland, 1994), 143.

(1-27) …the peopling of Australasia was an event of major importance for all humanity … it altered the course of evolution for our species.

The Future Eaters: An ecological history of the Australasian lands and people (Sydney: Reed New Holland, 1994), 155.

(1-28) …in the new land, every hunt would have been successful. Without predators and surrounded by naïve prey, people would have become, in a sense, gods. For they were now all-powerful beings in a land of plenty.

The Future Eaters: An ecological history of the Australasian lands and people (Sydney: Reed New Holland, 1994), 160.

JOSEPHINE FLOOD
On occupation of the highlands

(1-29) The basic way of life of recent hunter-gatherers in the Southern Uplands thus appears to have been established well before the end of the last glaciation, but the great change amidst this continuity was the move into the vastness of the mountains, a move that may have been prompted by the small brown Bogong moth.

The Moth Hunters: Aboriginal Prehistory of the Australian Alps (Canberra: Australian Institute of Aboriginal Studies, 1980), 283.

On Australian prehistory

(1-30) …Aboriginal society has the longest continuous cultural history in the world…

Archaeology of the Dreamtime: The story of prehistoric Australia and its people (Sydney: Collins, 1983), 16.

ERNEST GILES
On rock art in Central Australia

(1-31) We were over-run by ants, and pestered by flies, so in self-

defence we took another walk into the gullies, revisited the
aboriginal National Gallery of paintings and hieroglyphics,
and then returned to our shade and our ants.

Australia Twice Traversed, vol. 1 (London: S. Low, Marston, Searle &
Rivington, Limited, 1889), 101.

RICHARD A. GOULD
On the nomenclature of microlithic assemblages

(1-32) I propose that we discard the ambiguous term microlith in
favour of an hypothesis which will include all small stone
tools in Australia (that is, tools thought to be small enough
to have required hafting). This would be referred to as
the 'Australian small-tool tradition'. It includes, but is not
limited to backed blades.

'Puntutjarpa rockshelter: A reply to Messrs. Glover and Lampert',
Archaeology and Physical Anthropology in Oceania 4(3) (1969), 229-237,
234-235.

On desert subsistence

(1-33) In a sense the Aborigines eat their way into a camp by
first exploiting all the food resources near the surrounding
waterholes whenever possible before settling at the main
waterhole.

'Subsistence behavior among the Western Desert Aborigines of Australia',
Oceania 39 (1969), 253-274, 267.

J.W. (JOHN) GREGORY
On the abundance of discarded stone artefacts in the desert

(1-34) The fact is probably due to the stone-using people having
had no pockets.

*The Dead Heart of Australia: A Journey around Lake Eyre in the Summer of
1901-1902, with some account of the Lake Eyre basin and the flowing wells of
Central Australia* (London: John Murray, 1906), 77.

LESLEY HEAD
On the ecological impact of people

(1-35) The point here is to show how difficult it is, even in the colonisation scenario, to clearly separate human influences from climatic and other ones. Thus I have come to the conclusion that the term 'impact' should be reserved for meteorites and that the concept of 'interaction' is more useful.

'The (Aboriginal) face of the (Australian) earth', The Jack Golson Lecture series, Centre for Archaeological Research, Australian National University, 2006, 15.

On human vs climatic impacts

(1-36) In the big-man world of Australian archaeology the polarised 'human impacts' debates of the last twenty years or so have, presumably inadvertently, reinforced the false choice between ecological and social processes. There has been something of a sense that the space in the middle is for wimps who are not prepared to take a stand.

'The (Aboriginal) face of the (Australian) earth', Jack Golson lecture series, Centre for Archaeological Research, Australian National University, 2006, 19.

On extinction of the megafauna

(1-37) If we had the dating so well worked out that we knew the timing of the first human footstep, the first firestick and the very last Diprotodon, even if we had them all in the same site, we still would not have a causal explanation for the extinction unless we could demonstrate the mechanisms that connect them.

'The (Aboriginal) face of the (Australian) earth', Jack Golson lecture series, Centre for Archaeological Research, Australian National University, 2006, 17.

DAVID HORTON
On the social effects of megafauna

(1-38) If the megafauna had not become extinct, would Oxley,
Cunningham, and Mitchell, exploring the Liverpool Plains,
Darling Downs and western district of Victoria, have
simply encountered small groups of foragers … or, for this
was 'Diprotodon Country' … would they have found large,
structured groups with a clear authority structure and a
strong territorial sense?

'Seasons of repose: Environment and culture in the late Pleistocene of
Australia', in A. Aspimon (ed.), *The Pleistocene Perspective*, vol. 2 (London:
Allen & Unwin, 1986), 7-13, 11.

On the extinction of the megafauna

(1-39) But Australia's design is such that it has always been a close
call, the megafauna teetering on the edge of the table… The
end of the Pleistocene is that period of the smash then, the
environment an equivalent of the stock market crash of
1929. Just a little bit drier on the margins, the desert just a
bit bigger, just a few less active rivers and waterholes, and
there are massive impacts on a few species that had survived
hundreds of thousands of years of smaller fluctuations
previously. And the presence of humans is of no more
significance than that there was an audience for the losses.

*The Pure State of Nature: Sacred Cows, Destructive Myths and the
Environment* (St Leonards, NSW: Allen & Unwin, 2000), 122.

On defining the megafauna

(1-40) What is the 'megafauna'? They are the species that became
extinct at the end of the Pleistocene period. Anything else
about them? Anything suspicious?

*The Pure State of Nature: Sacred Cows, Destructive Myths and the
Environment* (St Leonards, NSW: Allen & Unwin, 2000), 113.

WALTER HOWCHIN
On finds at the mouth of the River Torrens

(1-41) At the time of the human occupation of the site, neither
the river nor the sea had covered the locality, which was
occupied by sand drifts, and it was on these sand hills
that the aboriginals were camped... These successive
changes require a considerable length of time for their
accomplishment and an undoubted antiquity for the human
remains.

'Supplementary notes on the occurrence of Aboriginal remains discovered
by Captain S.A. White at Fulham', *Transactions & Proceedings of the Royal
Society of South Australia* 43 (1919), 81-84, 84.

ALFRED W. HOWITT
On the antiquity of the Aborigines

(1-42) In considering all the facts before me bearing upon
the question of the origins of the Tasmanians and the
Australians, I have been much impressed by the immense
periods of time which seem to be essential as one of the
elements of any solution to the problem.

'On the origin of the Aborigines of Tasmania and Australia', *Australasian
Association for the Advancement of Science* 7 (1898), 723-58, 738.

CHRIS JOHNSON
On the vulnerability of the megafauna

(1-43) Wherever humans have harvested from their environment,
long-lived, slow-breeding and slow maturing species, living
in situations that guaranteed high exposure to people, have
been the most likely to disappear.

Australia's Mammal Extinctions: A 50,000 year history (Melbourne:
Cambridge University Press, 2006), 114.

RHYS JONES
On the initial entry into Australia

(1-44) No carefully equipped vessel this time, but some primitive canoe or log of wood. No Houston Control or Royal Society to report back to, for it was probably a one-way journey. Yet man had just joined the rat and the bat in crossing the great biological barrier of Wallacea…

'Editorial', *Mankind* 7 (1969), 81-82, 81.

On a submerged land bridge

(1-45) The first men to set foot on Rocky Cape may have toiled up the same rocky slope which in 1798 A.D. was kelp covered and murky, lying several fathoms beneath the gliding keel of the brig 'Norfolk'. Indeed without being too fanciful, the very reef that Flinders and Bass were careful to avoid may have been the vantage point which gave those first explorers their glimpse of the caves which were destined to shelter them and their descendants for the next eight millennia.

Rocky Cape and the Problem of the Tasmanians, PhD thesis, University of Sydney, 1971, 33.

On people as the decisive factor in extinction of the megafauna

(1-46) I am left with the thought that if man had *not* managed to cross the last water channel of Wallacea those distant tens of millennia ago, would our knowledge of the late Pleistocene 'giant marsupial' fauna only have come to us from the bone breccias of a Wellington Cave and the dusty golgothas of museums, or would at least some large beasts, lumbering down to the water's edge, have graced the sketchbooks of a Joseph Banks or a Charles Lesueur?

'The Neolithic, Palaeolithic and the hunting gardeners: man and land in the Antipodes', in R.P. Suggate and M. Cresswell (eds.), *Quaternary Studies* (Wellington: Royal Society of New Zealand, 1975), 21-34, 29-30.

On the Pleistocene settlement of Tasmania

(1-47) Twenty thousand years ago, the road to Tasmania lay open
and dry. Unlike Moses, the ancestral Tasmanians needed
no special divine act to facilitate their journey; rather the
glacio-eustatic lowering of the sea … exposed the floor
of the Bassian bridge, the critical sill linking island to
continent…

'Man as an element of a continental fauna: The case of the sundering
of the Bassian bridge', in J. Allen, J. Golson & R. Jones (eds.), *Sunda
and Sahul: Prehistoric Studies in Southeast Asia, Melanesia and Australia*
(London: Academic Press, 1977), 317-386, 374.

On the effects of cultural isolation

(1-48) Let us end with Tasmania and consider the trauma which
the severance of the Bassian bridge delivered to the
society isolated there. Like a blow above the heart, it took
a long time to take effect, but slowly but surely there was
a simplification of the tool kit, a diminution in the range
of foods eaten, perhaps a squeezing of intellectuality. The
world's longest isolation, the world's simplest technology.
Were 4000 people enough to propel forever the cultural
inheritance of Late Pleistocene Australia? Even if Abel
Tasman had not sailed the winds of the Roaring Forties
in 1642, were they in fact doomed – doomed to a slow
strangulation of the mind?

'The Tasmanian Paradox', in R.V.S. Wright (ed.), *Stone Tools as Cultural
Markers: change, evolution and complexity* (Canberra: Australian Institute
of Aboriginal Studies, 1977), 189-204, 203.

On the Rocky Cape site

(1-49) The bulk of the deposit consisted of the shells of coastal
gastropods, dumped there after having been collected and
eaten by prehistoric foragers. Within this matrix which was a
complex structure of interleaved and intercut elliptical hearths

and shell lenses, were bones of animals killed and cooked and also artefacts of bone and stone, the latter consisting of cores, waste flakes and formed tools. A chronologically ordered sequence, across this 8,000 year time span…

‘Hunting Forbears’, in M. Roe (ed.), *The Flow of Culture: Tasmania studies* (Canberra: Australian Academy of the Humanities, 1987), 14-49, 31-32.

RHYS JONES AND HARRY ALLEN
On Pleistocene flaked stone assemblages

(1-50) This assemblage, both in terms of the characteristics of its flaking and the types of implements present, is typical of other old Australian industries. We propose to call the cultural tradition to which they belong, the ‘Australian core tool and scraper tradition.’ The Mungo assemblage is the oldest evidence for it so far discovered in Australia.

J.M. Bowler, R. Jones, H. Allen, A.G. Thorne, ‘Pleistocene Human Remains from Australia: A Living Site and Human Cremation from Lake Mungo, Western New South Wales’, *World Archaeology* 2(1) (1970), 39-60, 52.

RHYS JONES AND TIA NEGEREVICH
On the Kakadu escarpment

(1-51) Along the base of the great cliffs which form the convoluted western edge, several hundred kilometres long, of the Arnhem Land plateau and of its numerous massive outliers, are rockshelters which constitute one of the world's most important storehouses of information about the prehistory and the art of hunting and gathering man. In terms of the number and age of the occupied shelters, and the profusion and antiquity of the rock art sites, the Kakadu area can be compared with … the Dordogne region of southwestern France.

‘A review of previous archaeological work’, in R. Jones (ed.), *Archaeological Research in Kakadu National Park* (Canberra: Australian National Parks and Wildlife Service, 1985), 1.

WILLIAM KEEGAN
On modeling the colonisation of Australia

(1-52) Archaeologists seem to face far more complications in making the crossing to Sahul than the people who accomplished this feat about 50 kya.

'Now bring me that horizon', comment on J.F. O'Connell and J. Allen, 'The restaurant at the end of the universe: Modelling the colonisation of Sahul', *Australian Archaeology* 74 (2012), 5-31, 22.

RON LAMPERT
On the settlement of Kangaroo Island

(1-53) For almost exactly a century after its discovery Kangaroo Island was thought never to have been occupied by people other than the Europeans who settled there. However, a stone industry of large core tools, found in 1902 as the land was being cleared by agricultural man, showed that the island had once harboured another human population.

'Kangaroo Island and the antiquity of Australians', in R.V.S. Wright (ed.), *Stone Tools as Cultural Markers: change, evolution and complexity* (Canberra: Australian Institute of Aboriginal Studies, 1977), 213-218, 213.

DOUGLAS LOCKWOOD
On archaeology in north Australia

(1-54) Well, the spades have been digging deep for years to discover something of our prehistory, primarily in Mediterranean countries ... I know of only one man, Jim Allen, who has put a scientist's pick in the North Australian ground.

My Old Mates And I (Adelaide: Rigby, 1979), 187.

HARRY LOURANDOS
On social and economic intensification

(1-55) The archaeologically sudden appearance of intensive and possibly ceremonially based occupation of marginal zones, for example wetlands, rainforests, highlands … and arid zones can be seen as an expansion of already developed and developing social networks into new ground.

'Intensification: A late Pleistocene-Holocene archaeological sequence from southwestern Victoria', *Archaeology in Oceania* 18 (1983), 81-94, 91.

(1-56) By all indications intensification of social and economic relations would appear to have been increasingly taking place during the Holocene period on the Australian mainland, the process being nipped in the bud by the coming of the Europeans.

'Intensification: A late Pleistocene-Holocene archaeological sequence from southwestern Victoria', *Archaeology in Oceania* 18 (1983), 81-94, 92.

ROGER LUEBBERS
On the recovery of ancient boomerangs 10,000 years old from peat in Wyrie swamp

(1-57) We can therefore see the Australian Aborigine emerging from the Pleistocene equipped with a tool kit as vital to the exploitation of the local environment then as it was yesterday, and just as complex. Exactly how long this technological tradition previously existed is as yet unknown but the possibility that the boomerang soared over the shores of Lake Mungo 16,000 years earlier seems more plausible as a result of discoveries at Wyrie Swamp.

'Ancient boomerangs discovered in South Australia', *Nature* 253 (1975), 39.

ISABEL MCBRYDE
On trading 'goods from another country'

(1-58) …it is clear that the major expeditions were not carried out simply for practical economic reasons. The contacts involved were important for their own sake, and materials bartered increased in social value as they passed through successive exchanges.

'Goods from another country: exchange networks and the people of the Lake Eyre basin', in D.J. Mulvaney and J.P. White (eds.), *Australians to 1788* (Sydney: Fairfax, Syme and Weldon, 1987), 253-273, 262.

On the great trade routes

(1-59) The desert itself thus shaped the patterns of relationships between the people who lived in its uncertain environment. Routes and destinations within the web of connection, hallowed by tradition and environmental necessity, figured prominently in mythologies describing the travels of ancestral beings in the Dreaming.

'Goods from another country: exchange networks and the people of the Lake Eyre basin', in D.J. Mulvaney and J.P. White (eds.), *Australians to 1788* (Sydney: Fairfax, Syme and Weldon, 1987), 253-273, 268.

N.W.G. 'BLACK MAC' MACINTOSH
On the Australian fossil evidence

(1-60) The mark of ancient Java is on all of them...

'The physical aspect of man in Australia', in R.M. Berndt and C.H. Berndt (eds.), *Aboriginal Man in Australia: essays in honour of Emeritus Prof. A.P. Elkin* (Sydney: Angus & Robertson, 1965), 29-70, 59.

KIM MAHOOD
On stone artefacts

(1-61) On the white sand lie fragments of worked stone, razor-edged flakes the colour of rust and amber... Each stone contains its own mystery, holding in itself the memory of the other hands which have held and crafted and discarded it.

Craft for a Dry Lake (Sydney: Anchor, 2000), 61.

BETTY MEEHAN
On shell middens as monuments

(1-62) The ubiquity of shell middens around the coasts of the world
may indeed be testimony to the special supportive role of
shellfish in coastal economies and be recognised as fitting
monuments to yet another unappreciated contribution made
by women to the maintenance of human society.

Shell Bed to Shell Midden (Canberra: Australian Institute of Aboriginal
Studies, 1982), 171-72.

MIKE MORWOOD
On the abundance of rock art in Australia

(1-63) Australia is the rock art capital of the world.

Visions from the past: the archaeology of Australian Aboriginal art (Crows
Nest, NSW: Allen & Unwin, 2003), 37.

JOHN MULVANEY
On the lack of archaeological data (in 1961)

(1-64) Australia remains the dark continent of prehistory even
after the passage of 170 years…

'The stone age of Australia', *Proceedings of the Prehistoric Society* 27 (1961),
56-107, 56.

On environmental conditions during the late Pleistocene

(1-65) …at that period, reliable rainfall extended across the heart
of the continent: Perennial rivers drained into inland seas
… there was a spread of rain-forest flora over the centre
of the continent… The luxuriant vegetation supported
a diversified and predominantly herbivorous land fauna.
Amongst the marsupials, most of the forms are now extinct,
but some belong to existing genera and most of them were
characterized by their tendency towards gigantism.

'The stone age of Australia', *Proceedings of the Prehistoric Society* 27 (1961),
56-107, 63.

On the paucity of stone artefacts

(1-66) The sample from this site is so small that definitive
judgements are impossible. For a so-called stone age people,
the aborigines were extraordinarily averse to using stone.

'Archaeological excavation of rock shelter no. 6, Fromm's Landing, South
Australia', *Proceedings of the Royal Society of Victoria* 77(2) (1964), 479-516,
492.

On the original explorers

(1-67) The discoverers, explorers and colonists of the three million
square miles which are Australia, were its Aborigines.

The Prehistory of Australia (New York: Praeger, 1969), 12.

On the rapid development of the field

(1-68) …archaeological research in Oceania emerged, only recently,
from the byways of antiquarianism and the haphazard
fringes of lunacy, into a vigorous and exciting discipline.

'Prehistory from Antipodean perspectives', *Proceedings of the Prehistoric
Society* 37(2) (1971), 228-252, 229.

On the rapid development of Australian archaeology

(1-69) That was 1961, the Dreamtime year for prehistory…

'Section III', in *Prehistory and heritage: the writings of John Mulvaney*
(Canberra: Department of Prehistory, ANU, 1990), 149-50, 149.

On the first ice age dates for occupation in Australia

(1-70) The results arrived by Royal Flying Doctor Service radio
one morning while we were camped at Kenniff Cave. I was
eating my breakfast of porridge and golden syrup while
[Reg] Orr checked the messages on his daily routine. A
message from Jean via Charleville provided a list of dates
for Kenniff back to 16000 years ago. Not anticipating such

an antiquity, I queried the result. Next morning's terse message from Jean confirmed the dates. To obtain the first stratified Pleistocene dates for human occupation, while digging the site, ranks as one of the most stimulating episodes of my career.

Digging Up a Past (Sydney: NewSouth Publishing, 2012), 113.

ANNIE NICHOLSON
On the paucity of evidence for marine exploitation on the southern coast

(1-71) …these coastal groups did not need to exploit sea foods to survive … they would appear to be desert people living on the coast; with their backs to the sea.

Archaeology on an arid coast: Environmental and cultural influences on subsistence economies on the west coast of South Australia, M.A. thesis, Australian National University, 1994, 130-131.

JIM O'CONNELL
On women in hunter-gatherer societies

(1-72) If women are archaeologically invisible in the Great Basin and Desert Australia, it is only because their economic presence is so large that we can't see the forest through the trees.

J. O'Connell, 2003, quoted in D.W. Bird and R.B. Bird, 'Evolutionary and Ecological Understandings of the Economics of Desert Societies: Comparing the Great Basin USA and the Australian Deserts', in P. Veth, M. Smith and P. Hiscock (eds.), *Desert peoples: archaeological perspectives* (Oxford: Blackwell, 2005), 81-99, 81-82.

ROBERT PULLEINE
On the prehistory of Rocky Cape

(1-73) Here the aborigines must have lived for ages, and if any light could be thrown on their culture by excavation, the

Rocky Cape talus offers the best deposit in all Tasmania. However, it is to be feared that excavation would be in vain as everything points to the conclusion that they were an unchanging people, living in an unchanging environment.

'The Tasmanians and their stone-culture', *Australasian Association for the Advancement of Science* 19 (1928), 294-314, 310.

ANDRÉE ROSENFELD
On archaic 'Panaramitee' petroglyphs

(1-74) ...the definition of a Panaramitee style as consisting of ancient non-figurative petroglyphs is seen to be both too wide, in its inclusion of material that is formally and structurally very diverse, and also too narrow in its insistence on restricted technology and likely age.

'Panaramitee: Dead or alive?', in P. Bahn and A. Rosenfeld (eds.), *Rock art and prehistory* (Oxford: Oxbow Books, 1991), 136-44, 143.

SAATCHI & SAATCHI AUSTRALIA
Advertisement capitalising on the new discoveries at Puritjarra

(1-75) After 20,000 years, Herbie Laughton Antjalka has no doubt Toyota are here for the long run. The Arrernte people were walking around the Red Centre at least 20,000 years ago. Now, for them, there's only one way to cross Australia's harsh and unforgiving desert. By Toyota.

Toyota Land Cruiser advertisement, *Weekend Australian*, 9-10 May 1992.

HAROLD L. SHEARD
On the results of a test pit at Devon Downs

(1-76) The floor to a depth of 3 feet is composed of ashes from old fires and a small amount of detritus from the cliff.

'Aboriginal rock carvings at Devon Downs', *Transactions of the Royal Society of South Australia* 51 (1927), 18-19, 18.

MIKE SMITH
On the fossil bird, *Genyornis*

(1-77) For such a large bird, taller than a man and weighing in at 275 kg, *Genyornis newtoni* is surprisingly difficult to find.

'Genyornis: last of the dromornithids', in L. Robin, R. Heinsohn and L. Joseph (eds.), *Boom and Bust: bird stories for a dry country* (Collingwood, VIC: CSIRO Publishing, 2009), 147-83, 147.

On the lack of change in stone tool assemblages

(1-78) The failure to generate a workable lithic systematics despite four decades of research into Australian Pleistocene assemblages suggests that stone flaking was an unreflexive daily practice, peripheral to the material culture and wider technology of these groups.

The archaeology of Australia's deserts (Cambridge: Cambridge University Press, 2013), 96.

WILLIAM J. SOLLAS
On comparing modern hunters with their presumed prehistoric counterparts

(1-79) Let us now turn to the Australians, the Mousterians of the Antipodes.

Ancient Hunters and Their Modern Representatives (London: Macmillan and co., 1911), 170.

On settlement of Australia

(1-80) …now they are confined to an isolated continent in the far south. It is tempting to suppose either that the inferior tribes of the Neandertal race were driven by stress of competition out of Europe, and wandered till they reached the Australian region; or that at some early time they occupied a tract of land extending almost continuously from Europe to Australia, and since been everywhere blotted out except in their southern home.

Ancient Hunters and Their Modern Representatives (London: Macmillan and co., 1911), 208.

E.C. (EDWARD) STIRLING
On the Lake Callabonna fossils

(1-81) There is, however, compensation for the unpromising physical features of Lake Callabonna in the fact that its bed proves to be a veritable necropolis of gigantic extinct marsupials and birds which have apparently died where they lie, literally in hundreds' mired in lake muds.

'The Physical features of Lake Callabonna', *Memoirs of the Royal Society of South Australia* 1 (1900), i-xv, i.

PETER THORLEY
On glacial maximum aridity

(1-82) …the glacial maximum provides the first and most crucial test of human adjustment to a truly arid environment … there is nothing that would have prepared them for the hyper-arid conditions of the last glacial maximum.

'Pleistocene settlement in the Australian arid zone: Occupation of an inland riverine landscape in the Central Australian ranges', *Antiquity* 72(275) (1998), 34-45, 42.

ALAN THORNE
On the Pacific Rim as a cultural arena in prehistory

(1-83) Suddenly, we see the Pacific basin as a single human universe, from Tasmania right round to Tierra del Fuego, created by a common process of evolution and expansion that began in mainland Asia. Despite all the differences in faces, skin colour, art, music, language, food and life-styles,

> there is a fundamental affinity, a sharing of origins, that
> binds them all.

A. Thorne and R. Raymond, *Man on the Rim: the Peopling of the Pacific*
(Sydney: Angus & Robertson, 1989), 8.

NORMAN B. TINDALE
On the Devon Downs-Tartanga dig

(1-84) In 1929 the consensus seemed to be that no cultural
changes were evident, and that the residence of the
Australian Aborigines had not extended far enough back
to have affected the ecology of the land. The Murray River
finds thus were a direct contradiction of prevailing ideas.

'A South Australian looks at some beginnings of archaeological research
in Australia', *Aboriginal History* 6 (1982), 92 110, 93.

On investigating the prehistoric settlement of Australia

(1-85) An appreciation of the ecology of the aborigines of
Australia is really an assessment of the ways of life, activities
and effectiveness of peoples of a series of palaeolithic
hunting tribal communities … drawn off from the whole
seething cauldron of Asia at various intervals of time…

'Ecology of primitive Aboriginal man in Australia', in A. Keast, R.L.
Crocker and C.S. Christian (eds.), *Biogeography and ecology in Australia*
(The Hague: Uitgeverij Dr W Junk, 1959), 36-51, 38-9.

BRUCE VEITCH
On the parallel use of grass seeds and Anadara bivalves

(1-86) The appearance of a widespread emphasis on r-selected
grass seeds in the archaeological record, associated with
the permanent occupation of much of the arid zone,
occurs at broadly the same time as the appearance of a
similar emphasis on r-selected bivalves along the northern
Australian coastline. This suggests a wider shift in many

regional economies towards increased emphasis on foods in the lower trophic levels.

'Shell middens on the Mitchell Plateau: A reflection of a wider phenomenon?', in J. Hall and I.J. McNiven (eds.), *Australian Coastal Archaeology*, Research Papers in Archaeology & Natural History 31 (Canberra: ANH Publications, ANU, 1999), 51-64, 53-54.

PETER VETH
On archaeological 'silence' in the arid northwest

(1-87) Have archaeologists, through flawed methodology and sample bias, managed to miss over 5000 years of the prehistory of northwest Australia? Is it simply chance that the complete absence of dates in this period coincides almost exactly with the timing of the height of the Last Glacial Maximum and the period immediately following? I think not.

'Aridity and settlement in northwest Australia', *Antiquity* 69(265) (1995), 733-746.

On modern humans and deserts

(1-88) Occupation of marginal landscapes such as deserts appears to be dated as early as other modern behaviors, such as the development of artistic expression, and the ability to make ocean crossings. This creates the fascinating scenario in which modern humans appear to have explored and colonized the world's deserts at the same time that they developed other 'modern' attributes underpinning a successful global diaspora, such as complex exchange and maritime skills.

'Conclusion: Major themes and future research directions', in P. Veth, M. Smith and P. Hiscock (eds.), *Desert peoples: archaeological perspectives* (Oxford: Blackwell, 2005), 299.

STEVE WEBB
On initial settlement of Australia

(1-89) Whatever initiated migration to Sahul, the most plausible model suggests that a slow, almost constant, trickle of people was needed to begin Australia's human story.

The First Boat People (Cambridge: Cambridge University Press, 2006), 111.

PAUL WENZ
On the lack of history

(1-90) There is no history; the childish primitive legends that peopled the great deserts died with the tribes. ... In Australia there is a total lack of ruins that are the tangible past, of the old castles and the old temples that form part of the history of a people.

Cited in Roslynn Haynes, *Seeking the Centre: The Australian Desert in Literature, Art and Film* (Cambridge: Cambridge University Press, 1998), 25.

J. PETER WHITE
On the potential of Australian archaeology

(1-91) Data wise, Australian prehistory is pretty marginal in the history of man; theoretically, it could be of immense significance.

'Back to 28,000 BC: Review of D.J. Mulvaney, Prehistory of Australia', *Nation*, 23 Aug 1969.

THOMAS WORSNOP
On the Anna Creek millstone quarry

(1-92) The quantity of stone removed from the Mount Douglas quarry equals 1,333 tons cubical measurement ... this quarry must have been worked for ages, and must have produced, allowing one-fourth for waste, some 71,000 stones for the use of the natives. This is the only quarry

for mill stones which has come under my own personal
observation; but I do not doubt that there are others of
a similar character in distant places, as the practice of
preparing food by this mode is almost universal amongst
the aborigines.

*The prehistoric arts, manufactures, works, weapons, etc., of the Aborigines of
Australia* (Adelaide: C.E. Bristow, Govt. Printer, 1897), 98.

R.V.S. (RICHARD) WRIGHT
On Koonalda Cave

(1-93) Koonalda Cave has a cool and awesome Gothic atmosphere
– gloomy cathedral-sized chambers, precipitous boulder
strewn slopes and mirror-smooth lake surfaces. The
immensity of its internal irregularity is heightened by
the monotony of the Plain outside. It was an impressive
adventure for each of us to stumble as far as the Squeeze
equipped with surveys, lights and the scientific knowledge
that the cave was merely a *natural* wonder. A thousand
feet underground is the evidence of the more courageous
prehistoric explorers.

'Preface', in R.V.S. Wright (ed.), *Archaeology of the Gallus Site, Koonalda
Cave*, Australian Aboriginal Studies 26 (Canberra: Australian Institute of
Aboriginal Studies, 1971), iii.

On the cessation of fishing in prehistoric Tasmania

(1-94) Any journal editor who sees a title which includes the
words 'Tasmania' and 'Fish' should reach for a gun.

attrib. Wright, 1982, in D. Horton, 'Here be dragons: A view of
Australian archaeology', in M.A. Smith, M. Spriggs and B. Fankhauser
(eds.), *Sahul in Review: Pleistocene archaeology in Australia, New Guinea
and Island Melanesia* (Canberra: Department of Prehistory, ANU, 1993),
11-16, 13.

2: ON THE PRACTICE OF ARCHAEOLOGY AND HISTORY

Local and international reflections on the tradecraft of archaeological practice.

ANON
On Norman Tindale's investigations at Devon Downs and Tartanga

(2-1) One thing we have needed badly is men of adequate training and ability who would roll up their shirt sleeves, spit on their hands, delve into the materials of aboriginal shelters and kitchen-middens…

The Australasian, 9 August 1930.

R.J.C. (RICHARD) ATKINSON
On looking beyond the finds

(2-2) The archaeologist has no right to that name unless he can look beyond his potsherds and post-holes to the only proper subject of his study, the men who made and used them.

Field Archaeology (London: Methuen, 1946), 177.

On the ideal excavation team

(2-3) …the navvy is to be preferred *for actual digging* to all but the most skilled and conscientious amateur … the ideal labour force for the small excavation consists of a few navvies with previous experience of archaeological digging, under a good foreman, and one or two experienced amateurs…

Field Archaeology (London: Methuen, 1946), 64.

PHILLIP BARKER
On the risk of small excavation trenches

(2-4) To dig holes, however well recorded, in an ancient site is like cutting pieces out of a hitherto unexamined manuscript, transcribing the fragments, and then destroying them, a practice which would reduce historians to an uncomprehending stupor, but whose counterpart is accepted by the majority of archaeologists as valid research.

Techniques of Archaeological Excavation (London: Batsford, 1993), 79.

On the tradecraft of archaeology

(2-5) In spite of highly sophisticated technologies, the trowel, the brush and the shovel are still the basic excavation tools, and the diggers, the draughtsmen and women, the supervisors, surveyors and photographers are still the most powerful and subtle recorders and interpreters that we have, and it is they who will produce the new evidence for the past which will modify our view of history and of ourselves.

Techniques of Archaeological Excavation (London: Batsford, 1993), 12.

Excavations as local history

(2-6) All excavations are local history. However widespread the ramifications of an excavation may ultimately prove to be, initially it is a piece of local history, embedded in the immediate landscape, and relating to the area around it.

Techniques of Archaeological Excavation (London: Batsford, 1993), 254.

WENDY BECK, ANNIE CLARKE AND LESLEY HEAD
On the predominance of women studying plant use

(2-7) …paleoethnofemobotantists…

'Preface', in *Plants in Australian Archaeology*, Tempus 1 (St. Lucia, QLD: Anthropology Museum, 1989), vi.

LEWIS BINFORD
On a running analysis

(2-8) Excavation must be conducted in terms of a running analysis and against a backdrop of the widest possible set of questions to which the data are potentially relevant. This is no technician's job.

'A Consideration of Archaeological Research Design', *American Antiquity* 29(4) (1964), 425-441, 440.

On an archaeology of place

(2-9) The archaeologist 'sees' the past segmentally from the perspective of fixed positions in space. The 'fallout' from the events that 'moved across' fixed places establishes the character of the archaeological remains on sites.

'The archaeology of place', *Journal of Anthropological Archaeology* 1 (1982), 5-13, 6.

SANDRA BOWDLER
On feminist analysis and a more humanistic archaeology

(2-10) …there is a creeping sterility in Australian archaeology, much of which stems from an environmentally/ecologically driven emphasis on 'behaviour' in a Skinnerian sense and a turning away from a more humanly oriented, ethnographically enriched archaeology. Feminist analysis is one way back towards a more humanistic archaeology, if not the only one.

'Review of Redefining Archaeology: Feminist Perspectives', *Archaeology in Oceania* 35(2) (2000), 94-95, 95.

DENIS BYRNE
On the pursuit of deep time

(2-11) If archaeology in Australia were to cease concerning itself with the nation's desire for 'depth' it might rise, as it were, to the surface.

'Deep nation: Australia's acquisition of an indigenous past', *Aboriginal History* 20 (1998), 82-107, 102.

THOMAS CARLYLE
On the collective nature of history

(2-12) History is the essence of innumerable biographies.

'On History' (1830), in Chris R. Vanden Bossche (ed.), *Thomas Carlyle: Historical Essays*, (Berkeley, CA: University of California Press, 2002), 5.

AGATHA CHRISTIE
A novelist's musings on her husband's profession

(2-13) As I look at it an archaeologist is a poor kind of fish. Always burrowing in the ground and talking through his hat about what happened thousands of years ago – and how do they know, I should like to know? Who's to contradict them? They say some rotten string of beads is five thousand three hundred and twenty-two years old, and who's to say it isn't? Well, there they are – liars, perhaps – though they seem to believe it themselves – but harmless.

Detective Chief Inspector James Japp discussing suspects with Hercule Poirot, *A Death in the Clouds* (London: Collins, 1973), 149-150.

GRAHAME CLARK
On the attraction of archaeology

(2-14) From the student's point of view one of the main attractions of prehistoric archaeology is the way it brings them even at an undergraduate level to the very brink of the unknown.

Prehistory at Cambridge and beyond (New York: Cambridge University Press, 1989), 15.

JEFFREY T. CLARK AND JOHN TERRELL
On identifying the crucial pieces of evidence

(2-15) If truth is the daughter of time, then the past is like a secretive woman of shady history. If left to her own devices, she will tell you nothing. If you attempt to piece her story together on your own, you will have to work from what she inadvertently lets you find. If asked directly, all she will say is 'What do you want to know?' If you hesitate a moment before answering, you will foresee the predicament she has trapped you in, because her next question will be the hardest one of all: What do you need to know?

'Archaeology in Oceania', *Annual Review of Anthropology* 7 (1978), 293-319, 314.

R.G. (ROBIN) COLLINGWOOD
On the importance of a clear objective

(2-16) ...long practice in excavation had taught me that one condition – indeed the most important condition – of success is that the person responsible for any piece of digging, however small and however large, should know exactly why he was doing it. He must first of all decide what he wants to find out, and then decide what kind of digging will show it to him.

An autobiography (Oxford: Oxford University Press, 1982), 121.

(2-17) I have been preaching to my archaeological friends the duty of never digging either a five-thousand-pound site or a five-shilling trench without being certain that you can satisfy an inquirer who asks you 'What are you doing this piece of work for?'

An autobiography (Oxford: Oxford University Press, 1982), 116.

On the history of thought

(2-18) …no historical problem should be studied without studying what I called its second-order history; that is, the history of historical thought about it … or the history of history…

An autobiography (Oxford: Oxford University Press, 1982), 132.

O.G.S. (OSBERT) CRAWFORD
On the qualities required of a field archaeologist

(2-19) Field-work does demand certain qualities – patience and perseverance, enthusiasm, constant scepticism and self-criticism. It requires and produces physical fitness and the ability to put up with some discomforts. One must be able to withstand the rigours of the British climate in winter and early spring, and of the British hotels at all seasons of the year.

Archaeology in the Field (London: Phoenix House, 1953), 59.

CHARLES DARWIN
On the importance of theory

(2-20) About thirty years ago there was much talk that geologists ought only to observe and not theorize; and I well remember someone saying that at this rate a man might as well go into a gravel-pit and count the pebbles and describe the colours. How odd it is that anyone should not see that all observation must be for or against some view to be of any service!

Charles Darwin to Henry Fawcett, 1861, cited in Donald R. Prothero, *Evolution: What the Fossils Say and Why It Matters* (New York: Columbia University Press, 2007), 4.

GREG DENING
On the importance of the scientific imagination

(2-21) The history in places, especially in places of cross-cultural encounters, will take as much imagination as science to see.

Blood and ashes are blown away with the dust. Shouts and songs die in the wind. Pain and happiness are as evanescent as memory. To catch the lost passions in places history will have to be a little more artful than being 'non-fiction'. It will have to have, among other graces, a trust in and a sense of the continuities of living through different times...

'The History in Things and Places', in T. Bonyhady and T. Griffiths (eds.), *Prehistory to politics: John Mulvaney, the humanities and the public intellectual* (Carlton South, VIC: Melbourne University Press, 1996), 85-97, 97.

On prehistory and archaeology

(2-22) Knowledge of this sort is hard won, full of claims and counter claims, zigzagging through a dozen disciplines. It is never static. There are no short cuts. It is a brilliant experience to be out there on the frontiers of knowledge. But it is a dangerous place to be.

'Living in and with deep time', *Journal of Historical Sociology* 18(4) (2005), 269-281, 270.

J.P. (JOHN) DROOP
On recording an excavation

(2-23) To take notes at an excavation is in itself an art to be learnt. It is not easy to write a description that shall omit nothing of importance and be intelligible to another person or to the writer himself six months afterwards when the context has faded from his mind.

Archaeological Excavation (Cambridge: Cambridge University Press, 1915), 27.

On mixed gender digs

(2-24) Of a mixed dig however I have seen something, and it is an experiment that I would be reluctant to try again; I would grant if need be that women are admirably fitted for the work, yet I would uphold that they should undertake it by themselves.

Archaeological Excavation (Cambridge: Cambridge University Press, 1915), 63.

KNUT FAEGRI AND JOHS IVERSEN
On pollen analysis

(2-25) …pollen analysis has been the dominant method for investigation of Late Quaternary development of vegetation and climate. It has been perfected into a very refined instrument of research, highly versatile and giving surprisingly intimate glimpses into the conditions of life during earlier periods. It has thus become one of the most important auxiliary sciences for archaeology, adding to the picture given by human relics.

Textbook of Pollen Analysis (Oxford: Blackwell, 1964), 12.

JOHN FERRY
On the role of theory

(2-26) I have no grand theory to peddle. I have no time for the 'pushers of systems'. I prefer to be nudged by theory rather than dominated by it.

Colonial Armidale (St Lucia, QLD: University of Queensland Press, 1999), 14.

KENT FLANNERY
On changing perspectives of Mesoamerican prehistoric farmers

(2-27) We no longer think of the preceramic plant-collectors as a ragged and scruffy band of nomads; instead, they appear as a practiced and ingenious team of lay botanists who know how to wring the most out of a superficially bleak environment. Nor do we still picture the Formative peoples as a happy group of little brown farmers dancing around their cornfields and thatched huts; we see them, rather, as a very complex series of competitive ethnic groups with internal social ranking and great preoccupation with status, iconography, water control, and the accumulation of luxury goods.

'Archaeological systems theory and early Mesoamerica', in S. Struever (ed.), *Prehistoric Agriculture* (Garden City, NY: Natural History Press, 1971), 80-100, 80.

On sampling

(2-28) I have to hand it to R. M. A. [Real Mesoamerican Archaeologist], because he turned that 5m of totally mixed mound fill into a seriated sequence of pottery types which looked – when presented as a graph of frequency polygons, or 'battleships' – totally convincing. ... Never have the aesthetic qualities of sampling error been more tastefully displayed.

The Early Mesoamerican Village (New York: Academic Press, 1976), 3.

On the 'Skeptical Graduate Student' (S.G.S.)

(2-29) He is obnoxiously smart, and has only a vestigial respect for established authority. Idealism sticks out all over him. His edges are rough. He understands the New Math. ... 'I've been reading Binford,' he began. I stiffened a little at that, because these religious fanatics always make me nervous. ... 'Do you know Binford personally?' he finally asked. 'Yes', I answered. 'I was with him the day he fed 5000 undergraduates with a few loaves of bread and a newspaperful of fish.'

The Early Mesoamerican Village (New York: Academic Press, 1976), 4.

On the fun of archaeology

(2-30) Hell, I don't break the soil periodically to 'reaffirm my status'. I do it because archaeology is still the most fun you can have with your pants on.

'The Golden Marshalltown: A Parable for the Archeology of the 1980s', *American Anthropologist* 84(2) (1982), 265-278, 278.

JOSEPHINE FLOOD
On the profession

(2-31) Australian archaeology has in its ranks a high number of hypercritical individuals…

'No ethnography, no moth hunters', in B. Meehan and R Jones (eds.), *Archaeology with Ethnography: An Australian Perspective* (Canberra: Australian National University, 1988), 270-276, 274.

On the role of ethnography

(2-32) …even though the archaeological evidence alone was extremely suggestive of moth hunting activities, it is still true to say 'no ethnography, no moth hunters'.

'No ethnography, no moth hunters', in B. Meehan and R Jones (eds.), *Archaeology with Ethnography: An Australian Perspective* (Canberra: Australian National University, 1988), 270-276, 274.

(2-33) The rich Australian ethnography describes a whole way of life whereas only a fragment has been preserved in the archaeological record. To ignore this would be like excavating sites in Roman Britain without reading Tacitus, or pre-Hellenic Greece without a glance at Homer.

The Moth Hunters: Aboriginal Prehistory of the Australian Alps (Canberra: Australian Institute of Aboriginal Studies, 1980), 23.

DAVID FRANKEL
On excavation as a creative process

(2-34) …excavators do not destroy archaeological sites; they create
them.

'The excavator: creator or destroyer?' *Antiquity* 67(257) (1993), 875-877, 875.

On the problem of small excavations

(2-35) If our successors are able to excavate so much better than
we can … They will have black holes of uncertainty in
the centre of their site-plans, and will curse us as much
for digging small portions of sites and destroying spatial
patterns as for digging the whole.

'The excavator: creator or destroyer?' *Antiquity* 67(257) (1993), 875-877, 876.

On the dynamic state of sites

(2-36) Sites are not stable. They will not remain unaltered, even if
we refrain from investigating them. Apart from immediate
and direct human threats, there are less easily controlled
forces at work – water, wind, rabbits and other agents of
destruction. Perhaps we have an obligation to excavate.

'The excavator: creator or destroyer?' *Antiquity* 67(257) (1993), 875-877,
877.

On excavation as transformation

(2-37) In terms of the processes that make and change sites and
knowledge, the excavator should be seen not simply as a
destroyer, but as a particular agent of transformation, which
creates our structured archaeological record.

'The excavator: creator or destroyer?' *Antiquity* 67(257) (1993), 875-877, 877.

RICHARD FULLAGAR
On the limitations of stone artefacts

(2-38) It seems preposterous that stone artefacts have anything
significant to tell us about culture especially in recent
Aboriginal Australia, where simple stone chips pale
to insignificance alongside the complex social life of
Aboriginal people. … The challenge is to further develop
ways of linking stone artefacts directly with the significant
questions about subsistence and resource use, settlement
mobility, exchange and ideology.

'Traces of Times Past: Stone Artefacts into Prehistory', *Australian
Archaeology* 39 (1994), 63-73, 64.

STEPHEN GALE
On the archaeological record at Cuckadoo 1 rockshelter

(2-39) …the sediments represented 'as much gap as sequence'…

attrib. S. Gale, in I. Davidson, S. Sutton and S. Gale, 'The human
occupation of Cuckadoo 1 rockshelter, northwest central Queensland',
in M.A. Smith, M. Spriggs and B. Fankhauser (eds.), *Sahul in Review:
Pleistocene archaeology in Australia, New Guinea and Island Melanesia*
(Canberra: Department of Prehistory, ANU, 1993), 164-172, 168.

CLIVE GAMBLE
On the opportunity for social history

(2-40) …while impressed by the virtuoso skills now evident in
the excavation of open and rock-shelter sites from the
Palaeolithic, I nonetheless have to ask, what is all this
precision in recording artifact coordinates and taphonomy
about? … Have we in fact run out of things to do and
questions to ask? I don't think so. What follows is partly an
experiment in asking how such precision will allow us to
move away from stomach-led and brain-dead explanations

and instead direct our analytical ingenuity to the richness of
the social data our evidence contains.

The Palaeolithic Societies of Europe (Cambridge: Cambridge University
Press, 1999), pxx-xxi.

EDMUND GILL
On unadorned facts

(2-41) …our so-called history consists of written records which
are but interpretations of selected events … the sand and
silt and clay from our harbour floor are unadorned facts
… these sediments are a river's trawlings of travel. They tell
where the river has been and what were the conditions of
travel.

'History from the Harbor Floor', *Port of Melbourne Quarterly* (Jan-Mar,
1949), 30-31.

IAN GLOVER AND RON LAMPERT
On how to dig a site

(2-42) …if time and labour are limited, dig a small hole carefully
rather than a big hole quickly; if you cannot screen the
deposit from a cave site, do not dig it.

'Puntutjarpa rockshelter excavation by R.A. Gould: a critical review',
Archaeology and Physical Anthropology in Oceania 4 (1969), 222-228, 222-3.

JACK GOLSON
On progress in Australian and PNG archaeology

(2-43) As for ideological predispositions, conventional historians
live very easily with the thought that each generation
rewrites history in the light of its concerns.

'The last days of Pompeii?', in M.A. Smith, M. Spriggs and B. Fankhauser
(eds.), *Sahul in Review: Pleistocene archaeology in Australia, New Guinea
and Island Melanesia* (Canberra: Department of Prehistory, ANU, 1993),
275-280, 278.

On the theoretical hyper-sophistication of the age

(2-44) ...I have no doubt exposed the threadbare state of
my theoretical undergarments. Given the theoretical
hypersophistication of the age ... I can only say, like the jazz
musician, Eubie Blake, interviewed on his 100th birthday,
'If I'd known I was gonna live this long, I'd have taken better
care of myself.'

'The last days of Pompeii?', in M.A. Smith, M. Spriggs and B. Fankhauser
(eds.), *Sahul in Review: Pleistocene archaeology in Australia, New Guinea
and Island Melanesia* (Canberra: Department of Prehistory, ANU, 1993),
275-280, 278.

TOM GRIFFITHS
On history-making as an everyday process

(2-45) History can take many forms. It can be constructed at the
dinner table, over the back fence, in parliament, in the streets,
and not just in the tutorial room, or at the scholar's desk.

Hunters and Collectors: The antiquarian imagination in Australia
(Cambridge: Cambridge University Press, 1996), 1.

On individualising history

(2-46) Naming people changes the kind of history we write.

'Foreword', in M.A. Smith, *Peopling the Cleland Hills* (Canberra:
Aboriginal History Inc., 2005), x.

RODNEY HALL
On integrating the detail with the whole

(2-47) Can you imagine how caring the forger must be, how exact
with his craft, how much in love with what he does? First
he must grasp what he is to achieve and then keep this
general understanding in mind while he goes over the parts
in finest detail. He must look into each detail to see details
within a detail. He has to love the whole piece in the act of

loving these details within details, otherwise he will never make a forger.

A dream more luminous than love: the Yandilli trilogy (Sydney: Picador Australia, 1994), 185.

PETER HISCOCK
On good writing

(2-48) …archaeology is at its best when it is simultaneously easily read, without unnecessary jargon and detail, yet reflects the weight of scientific research…

The archaeology of ancient Australia (London: Routledge, 2008), preface, xiii.

DAVID HORTON
On the role of theory

(2-49) From the outside, the difficult part of archaeology seems to be finding the facts – finding the right site, the right artefact, the right bones. It would seem that once we have all the 'facts' then the true story will be known – we can write prehistory as we write history, if only we can get enough facts… There are, however, few if any 'facts' in archaeology. What we are really doing is developing and testing theories and the process is never-ending.

Recovering the Tracks: The story of Australian archaeology (Canberra: Aboriginal Studies Press, 1991), 352.

IAN JOHNSON
On the need for more systematic excavation recording

(2-50) …excavation techniques have grown up piecemeal and have failed to come to grips with the difficult conditions posed by the undifferentiated sandy stratigraphies and low sedimentation rates typical of many Australian sites.

'Abstract', *The Getting of Data: A case study from the recent industries of Australia*, PhD thesis, Australian National University, 1979.

PHILIP JONES
On the insight of 'contact' objects

(2-51) …Aboriginal artefacts not only evoke another culture and
another time, but also carry substantial traces of encounters
between their original makers or owners and their collectors.
… Having brushed against both cultures they wear a double
patina, of ochre and rust.

Ochre and Rust: Artefacts and Encounters on Australian Frontiers (Kent
Town, SA: Wakefield Press, 2007), 1.

RHYS JONES
On the state of Australian theory in 1968

(2-52) The honeymoon is over. The new wave of Australian
archaeology is settling down comfortably to a premature
middle age… Let us not confuse the accumulation of raw
data with improved quality of thought. Simple-minded
archaeology is still simple minded, be it conceived over
a continent or over a parish… We should be in the van
of archaeological theory on hunter-gatherers, instead of
uncritically following the lead of others.

Editorial, *Mankind* 6 (1968), 535-536, 535.

On weighing up evidence for an early presence of people

(2-53) For unequivocal proof of human occupation, however, we
must be satisfied with nothing less than artifacts or human
remains found *in situ* under controlled conditions, and
the complications to the literature resulting from similar
circumstantial evidence … should make us wary of less
stringent criteria.

'The geographical background to the arrival of Man in Australia and
Tasmania,' *Archaeology & Physical Anthropology in Oceania* 3 (1968), 186-
215, 188-189.

On a coarse-grained archaeological exploration of the continent

(2-54) These are large and coarse-grained questions, yet highly important and reproducible results have been obtained on a continent-wide scale precisely by the deployment of a strategy of excavating small pits in well chosen sites but with standards of data retrieval and recording, backed by geo-chronological, geomorphological, palynological and faunal analyses. The aim of this work has been primarily diachronic, to take a slice through time answering a series of interrelated questions which might be paraphrased as belonging to the 'who was where, when and what was the weather like?' school.

'Different strokes for different folks: Sites, Scale and Strategy', in I. Johnson (ed.), *Holier than thou: Proceedings of the 1978 Kioloa conference on Australian Prehistory* (Canberra: Department of Prehistory, ANU, 1980), 151-71, 151-2.

On archaeology in 'the obdurate continent'

(2-55) ...it is important not to underestimate the sheer brute difficulty of carrying out meaningful field prehistoric research in Australian conditions unless one has the full panoply of modern scientific methods at one's disposal. ... The Australian landscape is in general terms ungenerous to the archaeologist.

'A continental reconnaissance: some observations concerning the discovery of the Pleistocene archaeology of Australia', in M. Spriggs (ed.), *A community of culture: the people and prehistory of the Pacific* (Canberra: Department of Prehistory, ANU, 1993), 97-122, 104-105.

JOHAN KAMMINGA AND HARRY ALLEN
On the relationships between sites

(2-56) Archaeologists no longer construct chronological and 'cultural' sequences, supposedly relevant for a wide area, on evidence from excavations at single sites. One of the major concerns now is to detail the inter-relationships *between* sites, and, where possible, the country around them.

Alligator Rivers environmental fact finding study: report of the archaeological survey (Darwin: Government Printer for Alligator Rivers Region Environmental Fact-Finding Study, 1973), 110.

CLAUDE LÉVI-STRAUSS
On the perils of salvage ethnography

(2-57) While I complain of being able to glimpse no more than the shadow of the past, I may be insensitive to reality as it is taking shape at this very moment, since I have not reached the stage of development at which I would be capable of perceiving it. A few hundred years hence, in this same place, another traveller, as despairing as myself, will mourn the disappearance of what I might have seen, but failed to see.

Tristes Tropiques (World on the Wane), transl. by J. Russell (London: Hutchinson, 1961), 43.

On field work

(2-58) I hate travelling and explorers … Adventure has no place in the anthropologists' profession; it is merely one of those unavoidable drawbacks, which detract from his effective work through the incidental loss of weeks or months…

Tristes Tropiques (World on the Wane), transl. by J. Russell (London: Hutchinson, 1961), 27.

ISABEL MCBRYDE
On the development of the field

(2-59) So we may say that a new phase in archaeological research is beginning in Australia … an approach based on controlled stratigraphic excavation and systematic survey work, rather than random digging and collecting.

'Archaeology in Australia – some recent developments', *The Record* 6(1) (Mar 1964), 5-7, 5.

On the destruction of prehistoric sites

(2-60) Occupation sites in Australia (middens, rock shelters and open stations) are not so numerous that we can afford to be prodigal with them, to allow them to be destroyed ... to be dug carelessly by treasure-hunters whose sole interest is the collection of curious relics for the family mantelpiece.

'Archaeology in Australia – some recent developments', *The Record* 6(1) (Mar 1964), 5-7, 7.

On communities and regional histories

(2-61) From archaeological evidence ... we may ask two differing sets of questions. The first relates to the life of the site itself, as a source of information on the activities of the small community of people who lived there... However, of the material from each site, or each group of sites, we must also ask questions relating to the cultural history of the region as a whole. ... So one's small community of hunter-gatherers is studied, not as an important entity in itself, but as a reflection of a larger unit, the culture and life of the people of that region at a particular point in time.

Aboriginal Prehistory in New England (Sydney: Sydney University Press, 1974), 333.

On the importance of site studies

(2-62) In concentrating on a study of site sequences and their wider implications and relationships with those of other regions, it is easy to neglect the questions which relate to the community and its daily life. These questions have equal validity for the understanding of prehistory as concerned with historical problems.

Aboriginal Prehistory in New England (Sydney: Sydney University Press, 1974), 334.

KIM MCKENZIE
On the domestic perils of fieldwork

(2-63) I go home to present myself with accustomed uncertainty.

Unpublished comment, 'Lake Eyre basin symposium', Maree SA, 1988.

JOHN MCPHEE
On stratigraphy

(2-64) I didn't know until recently that stratigraphy is dead. Many schools don't teach it anymore. To me, that's writing the story without knowing the alphabet. The geologic literature is a graveyard of skeletons who worked the structure of mountain ranges without knowing the stratigraphy.

Annals of the Former World (New York: Farrar, Straus and Giroux, 1998), 385.

MAX MALLOWAN
On the grand days of archaeological exploration

(2-65) I have been fortunate to practise in what the late Sir Frederick Kenyon once described as 'the Elizabethan Age of Archaeology'. In the Orient we had, at least for the first three decades of my career, both the time and the financial resources to dig in the grand manner, on a grand scale … But given the restrictions of our present economy, no less than the development in scientific methods, we are bound to dig on a relatively modest scale and consequently to put all the evidence through a fine sieve: we therefore miss nothing, and tend to find nothing. Sometimes the evidence recovered is of so light a character that an older generation is inclined to wonder if the effort is worthwhile.

Mallowan's Memoirs: The autobiography of Max Mallowan (London: Collins, 1977), 302.

LESLEY MAYNARD
On the trials of day-to-day site recording

(2-66) Day by dreary day…

'Day by dreary day: a few jottings from the Aboriginal Relics diary', *Napawi* 2 (1973), 6-8.

VINCENT MEGAW
On the importance of publication

(2-67) Excavation without publication is, one might add, a combination of murder and criminal censorship. The machinery is there; only laziness, or poor planning of our work programmes – and I trust not lack of good-will – stands in the way.

'Australian Archaeology: how far have we progressed?', *Mankind* 6(7) (1966), 306-12, 308.

JOHN MULVANEY
On stratigraphy

(2-68) …the cornerstone of prehistory is stratigraphy, and in this pioneering phase of Australian research, precedence must be given to the spade (or preferably the trowel).

'Antiquity of man in Australia: prehistory', in H. Sheils (ed.), *Australian Aboriginal Studies: Conference on Aboriginal Studies, May 1961* (Melbourne: Oxford University Press, 1963), 33-51, 37.

On the need for fieldwork before theory

(2-69) It is worth reflecting that new approaches to explicating the past, involving model formulation, theoretical constructs and trendy jargon, arose in continents with an archaeological data base and fieldwork traditions extending back over a century. Australians sometimes are criticised for their pragmatism and neglect of abstractions. At this juncture in archaeological research, however, there is much point in recording the mundane.

'Foreword – Archaeology in Queensland', *Queensland Archaeological Research* 1 (1984), 4-7, 4.

On discovery of late Pleistocene occupation at Kenniff Cave

(2-70) Chance, linked with a hunch, would not constitute a respectable research design today, yet that combination sufficed to discover a major site which both solved and posed problems of continental application.

'Foreword – Archaeology in Queensland', *Queensland Archaeological Research* 1 (1984), 4-7, 5.

On his own 'prehistory'

(2-71) I hankered after the Iron Age but knew I must return to Stone.

'Archaeological Retrospect 9', *Antiquity* 60(229) (1986), 96-107, 98.

TIM MURRAY
On the professionalisation of Australian archaeology

(2-72) …debates about innovation reveal much about the 'culture' of Australian prehistoric archaeology, specifically about the consequences of its recent professionalisation by a small founding population.

'Aboriginal (pre)history and Australian archaeology: The discourse of Australian prehistoric archaeology', *Journal of Australian Studies* 16(35) (1992), 1-19, 8.

JIM O'CONNELL
On the austerity of the Pleistocene archaeological record

(2-73) Research on the prehistory of Pleistocene Sahul will always
be challenging: the austerity of its archaeological record
guarantees it.

'An Emu hunt', in A. Anderson and T. Murray (eds.), *Australian
Archaeologist: collected papers in honour of Jim Allen* (Canberra: Coombs
Academic Publishing, ANU, 2000), 172-81, 179.

MARK O'CONNOR
On the rhythm and pace of archaeology

(2-74) Archaeology
Is not one-day cricket but a decades-long test;
Quick conceptions, then a long slow fostering
Of evidence, like rearing and training a wicked child.
A few weeks romance and dig,
Then that long monogamy of writing-up.

'Desert archaeology', Quadrant 58(9) (Sep 2014), 50-53, 51.

W.M. FLINDERS PETRIE
On museum collections

(2-75) Our museums are ghastly charnel-houses of murdered
evidence; the dry bones of objects are there, bare of all the
facts of grouping, locality, and dating which would give
them historical life and value.

Methods and Aims in Archaeology (London: Macmillan, 1904), 48.

V.S. (VICTOR) PRITCHETT
Said of Edward Gibbon

(2-76) Sooner or later, the great men turn out to be all alike. They never stop working. They never lose a minute. It is very depressing.

'Edward Gibbon Gibbon and the Home Guard', in V.S. Pritchett, *The complete essays* (London: Chatto & Windus, 1991), 1-16, 4.

LYDIA V. PYNE AND STEPHEN J. PYNE
On the importance of narrative

(2-77) For narrative to shape such meaning requires well-defined beginnings and endings. Paradoxically, a reliance on 'the science' may actually destabalise such a narrative. Build on the sands of data, and you will be swept away by the next flash flood of discovery. … Hypotheses are as disposable as laboratory pipettes; today's positivist theories become tomorrow's folktakes. To be powerful, a narrative must be anchored in art and philosophy, since aesthetic closure and moral resolution are what convey the context that endows facts with enduring meaning.

The Last Lost World: Ice Ages, Human Origins, and the Invention of the Pleistocene (New York: Viking, 2012), 37.

ANDRÉE ROSENFELD
On rock art research

(2-78) Rock art research is a field with a lunatic core and a sane fringe.

Andree Rosenfeld to Mike Smith, *pers. comm.* at Puritjarra, 1990.

SIMON SCHAMA
On the disruption of history

(2-79) …history clings tight but it also kicks loose. Disruption as much as persistence, is its proper subject.

A history of Britain: at the edge of the world? 3000 BC-AD 1603 (London: BBC, 2000) 10.

CARMEL SCHRIRE
On becoming an archaeologist

(2-80) I became an archaeologist because I wanted to drive around in a big Landrover, smoking, cursing, and finding treasure. During my fieldwork in Australia and South Africa, I managed to do all of these things, but as with all archaeological work, more time was spent washing, counting, and grouping the finds than getting them out of the ground.

Digging through Darkness: Chronicles of an Archaeologist (Charlottesville: University Press of Virginia, 1995), 71.

On the archaeological imagination

(2-81) Only imagination fleshes out the sound and taste of time past, anchoring the flavor of lost moments in the welter of objects left behind.

Digging through Darkness: Chronicles of an Archaeologist (Charlottesville: University Press of Virginia, 1995), 11.

WILFRED SHAWCROSS
On ethnographic analogy

(2-82) ...the difficulty may lie in the baggage of assumptions and impressions that the Australian archaeologist carries along with terms such as 'campsite'. ... It is surely one of the lessons of anthropology that culture is a dynamic process, not something fixed for all time. Is it not likely that the Pleistocene ancestors of the Aborigines did things differently?

'Archaeological Excavations at Mungo', *Archaeology in Oceania* 33(3) (1998), 183-200, 199.

MARY SHELLEY
On ambition and big science

(2-83) It was very different when the masters of science sought immortality and power; such views, although futile, were grand: but now the scene was changed. The ambition of the inquirer seemed to limit itself to the annihilation of those visions on which my interest in science was chiefly founded. I was required to exchange chimeras of boundless grandeur for realities of little worth.

Frankenstein, or the Modern Prometheus (Cambridge: Sever, Francis, & Co., 1869), 37.

BERNARD SMITH
On the sensuous enjoyment of material things

(2-84) …we need in this country not only the temperament that is capable of a direct sensuous response to material things, but also the temperament which is aware of the degree to which things have shaped our heritage. …Australasian historians may be encouraged to seek a more balanced, a more archaeological, a more humanist view of our history.

'History and the Collector' (1974), in *The Death of the Artist as Hero: Essays in History and Culture* (Melbourne: Oxford University Press, 1988), 97-98.

MIKE SMITH
On deductivism and empiricism in Australian archaeology

(2-85) No doubt the philosophers who sat and pondered on the number of teeth in a horse's mouth, based on the nature of the animal, were sterling deductivists and the lad who suggested that they find a horse and count its teeth, a naive empiricist. However this parable does serve to illustrate a familiar situation in archaeology.

'Central Australia: Preliminary Archaeological Investigations', *Australian Archaeology* 16 (1983), 27-38, 27.

On moving from the detail to the big picture

(2-86) We should not feel guilty if we allow ourselves to wallow in the minutiae of the archaeological record, but … we need to marry this with an eye for the big picture. A site like Puritjarra is not just sequence and chronology, but also a dynamic part of landscape – a place on someone's itinerary as they moved across western central Australia, stepping out across the desert.

'Reading Puritjarra', in M. Martin, L. Robin and M.A. Smith (eds.), *Strata: Deserts past, present and future* (Mandurama, NSW: Mandy Martin, 2005), 19-24, 22.

On shaping archaeology as a field

(2-87) …our discipline is shaped by each of us. It grows out of every day practise. It is what we make it and re-make it every day.

'Andrée Rosenfeld: A steadying influence on rock art research', talk at Memorial for Andrée Rosenfeld, University House, ANU, 2009.

WILLIAM SMITH
On biostratigraphy

(2-88) Organised fossils are to the naturalist as coins to the antiquary; they are the antiquities of the earth, and very distinctly show its gradual regular formation.

Stratigraphical system of organised fossils (London: Williams, 1817), ix-x.

DONALD F. THOMSON
On the Wik-Monkan Aboriginal people on Cape York Peninsula

(2-89) …little would remain to suggest to an archaeologist of the future, forced to depend upon examination of old camp sites and such artefacts as resisted decay, the extent and the complexity of the culture.

'The seasonal factor in human culture', *Proceedings of the Prehistoric Society* 5(2) (1939), 209-21, 209.

NORMAN B. TINDALE
On using ethnography

(2-90) How many of todays' great archaeologists have spent time working with native peoples on the subject of stone knapping? …it is high time that at least a few archaeologists should take note of Australian and New Guinea stone knappers and temporarily at least emerge from their cave holes to study at first hand the data provided by living peoples. … Surely if we work from known bases better results must follow than if we adopt what seems to be a very prevalent myopic attitude. 'Emus with their heads in the spinifex.'

'Stone Implement Making among the Nakako, Ngadadjara and Pitjandjara of the Great Western Desert', *Records of the South Australian Museum* 15(1) (1965), 131-64, 162-63.

HELEN TOLCHER
On an apprentice archaeologist

(2-91) …he was to be found on the edge of every interesting conversation, soaking up information like a sponge; on the site he was a patient and diligent worker who did whatever job he was given without complaint.

'In search of the Ngaiawang: The Roonka excavations 1968-1976', in K. Walshe (ed.), *Roonka: Fugitive Traces and Climate Mischief* (Adelaide: South Australian Museum, 2009), 106.

R.E.M. (MORTIMER) WHEELER
On interpreting stratigraphy

(2-92) It is not enough to identify layers … it is the task of the
archaeologist to interpret them, to understand the sentence
as well as to transliterate it.

Archaeology from the Earth (Oxford: Oxford University Press, 1954), 44.

(2-93) The reading of a section is the reading of a language that
can only be learned by demonstration and experience…
However practised, do not read too hastily.

Archaeology from the Earth (Oxford: Oxford University Press, 1954), 49.

On the importance of people in archaeology

(2-94) In a simple direct sense, archaeology is a science that
must be lived, must be 'seasoned with humanity.' Dead
archaeology is the driest dust that blows.

Still Digging (New York: E.P. Dutton & Co., 1956), 13.

J. PETER WHITE
On research

(2-95) Research is incomplete until it is written up, read, evaluated
and incorporated into our corpus of knowledge.

Note following Editorial, *Mankind* 7 (1969), 82.

J. PETER WHITE AND JIM O'CONNELL
On the importance of understanding the history of research

(2-96) …an historian must try to see what problems a past
individual faced and how these were solved … a fuller
appreciation of the nature and uniqueness of Sahul's
prehistory will derive from watching our predecessors solve
and fail to solve their problems.

A Prehistory of Australia, New Guinea & Sahul (Sydney: Academic Press,
1982), 30.

OSCAR WILDE
On archaeology and art

(2-97) For archaeology, being a science, is neither good nor
bad, but a fact simply. Its value depends entirely on how
it is used, and only an artist can use it. We look to the
archaeologist for the materials, to the artist for the method.
… Indeed archaeology is only really delightful when
transfused into some form of art.

'The Truth of Masks' (1891), in *Collected Works of Oscar Wilde*
(Hertfordshire: Wordsworth Editions Limited, 2007), 1017-1038, 1027-
1028.

GORDON WILLEY
On settlement patterns

(2-98) The material remains of past civilizations are like shells
beached by the retreating sea. The functioning organisms
and the milieu in which they lived have vanished, leaving
the dead and empty forms behind. An understanding of the
structure and function of ancient societies must be based
upon these static moulds which bear only the imprint of
life. Of all of those aspects of man's prehistory which are
available to the archaeologist, perhaps the most profitable
for such an understanding are settlement patterns.

Prehistoric settlement patterns in the Viru valley, Peru (Washington: U.S.
Govt. Print. Off., 1953), xviii.

H. MARTIN WOBST
On the tyranny of the ethnographic record

(2-99) Many of the constructs of space, time and behavior in the
ethnographic literature on hunter-gatherers may be partly
determined by the severe constraints on ethnographic

fieldwork. ... Their application to the archaeological record
may merely be ethnography with a shovel...

'The Archaeo-Ethnology of Hunter-Gatherers or the Tyranny of the
Ethnographic Record in Archaeology', *American Antiquity* 43(2) (1978),
303-309, 303.

LEONARD WOOLLEY
On the rhythm of an archaeological dig

(2-100) There *is* a romance in digging, but for all that it is a trade
wherein long periods of steady work are only occasionally
broken by a sensational discovery, and even then the
real success of the season depends, as a rule, not on the
rare 'find' that loomed so large for the moment, but on
the information drawn with time and patience out of a
mass of petty detail which the days' routine little by little
brought to light and set in due perspective.

Dead towns and living men: being pages from an antiquary's notebook
(London: J. Cape 1932), 2.

R.V.S. (RICHARD) WRIGHT
On the recycling and progression of ideas

(2-101) If we admit to hedonistic motives in our own work we can
be entertained and not threatened when we realise that
many of today's archaeological researches are refurbished
antiques.

'Introduction and two studies', in R.V.S. Wright (ed.), *Stone Tools as
Cultural Markers: change, evolution and complexity* (Canberra: Australian
Institute of Aboriginal Studies, 1977), 1-3, 3.

3: CHRONOLOGY, SEQUENCE AND PERCEPTIONS OF TIME

Deep time is a special preoccupation of the field of archaeology. These quotations explore the difficulties of dating – and imagining – time-spans covering thousands of years.

JAMES R. ARNOLD AND WILLARD F. LIBBY
On the discovery of radiocarbon dating

(3-1)These results seem sufficiently encouraging to warrant further investigation and application of the method.

'Age Determinations by Radiocarbon Content: Checks with Samples of Known Age', *Science* 110 (1949), 678-680, 680.

ROBERT BOYLE
On anticipating the discovery of thermoluminescence dating

(3-2) Observations made this 27th of October, 1663, about Mr. Clayton's Diamond … I also brought it to some kind of Glimmering Light, by taking it into Bed with me, and holding it a good while upon a warm part of my Naked Body.

The Works of the Honourable Robert Boyle, vol. 1 (London: printed for J. Rivington et al., 1772), 796-97.

THOMAS CARLYLE
On the brevity of a life

(3-3) One Life; a little gleam of Time between two Eternities.

On Heroes, Hero Worship and the Heroic in History (Boston: Ginn, 1901), 177-224, 203.

VERE GORDON CHILDE
On radiometric dating as a challenge to the tradecraft of archaeology

(3-4) …a mere archaeologist feels that the method will require considerable checking and refinement before it can provide reliable dates for prehistoric events.

'Comparison of archaeological and radiocarbon datings', *Nature* 166 (1950), 1068-69.

O.G.S. (OSBERT) CRAWFORD
On a historical perspective

(3-5) The archaeologist sees man as a time-product and his culture as an intermittent time-phenomenon… Time-thinking is an art that can be acquired…

Archaeology in the Field (London: Phoenix House, 1953), 43.

ELEANOR DARK
On a new 'settler' society, one without the framework of history

(3-6) The Timeless Land

Book title, historical novel, *The Timeless Land* (New York: Macmillan, 1941).

BRUNO DAVID
On historicising the Dreaming

(3-7) The Dreamtime is not so much ancient as timeless. … But like all things cultural, the Dreaming must have a history: it must have arisen out of human practice some time in the past. And in the Dreaming, as Aboriginal world-views of recent, ethnographic times emerged through the course of history, there surely were times in the past when Aboriginal people thought differently about the world.

Landscapes, rock-art and the Dreaming: an archaeology of preunderstanding (London: Leicester University Press, 2002), 1.

T.W. EDGEWORTH DAVID
On the discovery of the Talgai cranium

(3-8) Now, if we are asked 'Is man a geological antiquity in
Australia?' we can reply 'Yes, he is.'

David in T.W.E. David and J.T. Wilson, 'Preliminary communication on
an Australian cranium of probable Pleistocene age', *Report of the Eighty-
Fourth Meeting of the British Association for the Advancement of Science,
Australia: 1914, July 28-August 31* (London: John Murray, 1915), 531.

CHARLES DARWIN
On the geological record

(3-9) ...I look at the natural geological record as a history of the
world imperfectly kept, and written in a changing dialect; of
this history we possess the last volume alone, relating only
to two or three countries. Of this volume, only here and
there a short chapter has been preserved; and of each, only
here and there a few lines.

The Origin of Species (New York: P.F. Collier, 1909), 363.

GREG DENING
On time

(3-10) Time is in a section of a fish's ear-bone, time is the rings of
growth on a tree; time is pollen count; time is the character
of sands in a dune.

'Living in and with deep time', *Journal of Historical Sociology* 18(4) (2005),
269-281, 270.

LOREN EISELEY
On the archaeological eye

(3-11) A man who has once looked with the archaeological eye
will never see quite normally. He will be wounded by what
other men call trifles. It is possible to refine the sense of time
until an old shoe in the bunch grass or a pile of 19th century
bottles in an abandoned mining town tolls in one's head
like a hall clock. This is a price one pays for learning to read

time from surfaces other than the illustrated dial. It is the melancholy secret of the artifact, the humanly touched thing.

The Night Country (New York: Scribner, 1971), 81.

ROBERT ETHERIDGE
On evidence for the antiquity of humans in Australia

(3-12) The question has frequently presented itself – Are there any geological traces of man on this Continent, such as exist in other countries, and whereby the presence of a former race, or the antiquity of the present fast disappearing one, can be traced? The answer given by those most competent to judge is – No!

'Has man a geological history in Australia', *Proceedings of the Linnean Society of New South Wales* 5 (1890), 259-266, 259.

TIM FLANNERY
On the disproportionate effects of contamination on older ^{14}C samples

(3-13) Unless the amount of contamination is massive, it is not such a problem for samples less than 20 000 years old… It is a bit like being one dollar out when counting a thousand. But contamination can be a very severe problem for very old samples, when so few atoms are being counted. The contamination may then be like miscounting by a dollar when there are only two dollars!

The Future Eaters: An ecological history of the Australasian lands and people (Sydney: Reed New Holland, 1994), 151.

JOHN FRERE
On the idea of an ice-age world

(3-14) …a very remote period indeed; even beyond that of the present world.

J. Frere, 1800, cited in G. Daniel, *A Hundred and Fifty Years of Archaeology* (London: Duckworth, 1975), 27.

CLIVE GAMBLE
On timewalking

(3-15) Wareen, the cave of the wombat, had last been used 18,000 years ago when its roof collapsed during the height of the last global ice age. ... Levering himself out of the narrow trench one day, the team's leader Professor Jim Allen called me over. 'There's timewalking for you,' he said. 'One foot at 25,000 B.C. and other on A.D. 1990. That's why prehistory is special. Put that in your book.'

Timewalkers: The prehistory of global colonisation (London: Alan Sutton, 1993), x.

On the benefits of a radiocarbon chronology

(3-16) Australian archaeologists made full use of the advent of radiocarbon to unravel its prehistory and so largely escaped from the straitjacket imposed by flint typologies and their arguments of lithic ancestry.

Timewalkers: The prehistory of global colonisation (London: Alan Sutton, 1993), 215.

EDMUND GILL
On radiocarbon dating

(3-17) The Atom Bomb so fills the news that we seldom hear of the other results of radio-activity.

'*Measuring Age by Radiocarbon*', undated manuscript in Gill Papers, Museum of Victoria.

GRAHAM GREENE
On the geography of the mind

(3-18) The imagination has its own geography which alters with the centuries.

'The Explorers' (1952), in *Collected Essays* (Harmondsworth: Penguin, 1970), 237.

TOM GRIFFITHS
On ice as an archive of deep time

(3-19) When you drill into an ice cap that is kilometres thick, you can extract a core that is layered year by year, a precious archive of deep time. Ice cores are the holy scripts, the sacred scrolls of our age.

'A Humanist on Thin Ice', *Griffith REVIEW* 29 (2010), 67-117, 73.

LESLEY HEAD
On deep time

(3-20) Deep time – the awareness of the immensity of the past and the quick flash of history – became accepted among scholars at least between the mid-seventeenth and early eighteenth centuries.

Second Nature: the history and implications of Australia as Aboriginal landscape (Syracuse, NY: Syracuse University Press, 2000), 91-92.

On the value of time

(3-21) Changes in the numbers rewrite a certain kind of history, but it is not the only interesting or important one.

'Headlines and Songlines', *Meanjin* 55(4) (1996), 736-743, 743.

DAVID HORTON
On comprehending time

(3-22) If a slip of a trowel can remove a few hundred years of deposit, it is hard to comprehend the slowness of the process that laid down those sediments. … We have become blasé about time…

'Here be dragons: A view of Australian archaeology', in M.A. Smith, M. Spriggs and B. Fankhauser (eds.), *Sahul in Review: Pleistocene archaeology in Australia, New Guinea and Island Melanesia* (Canberra: Department of Prehistory, ANU, 1993), 11-16, 12.

(3-23) …we can hear the clink of spade on hearth, hear the scrap bucket emptied, day after day, month after month, year after year. … 'One kyr' it should be remembered is about 50 generations, an unimaginable sequence of births, lives and deaths.

'Here be dragons: A view of Australian archaeology', in M.A. Smith, M. Spriggs and B. Fankhauser (eds.), *Sahul in Review: Pleistocene archaeology in Australia, New Guinea and Island Melanesia* (Canberra: Department of Prehistory, ANU, 1993), 11-16, 12.

On what the immensity of time really means

(3-24) In the roll of that phrase 'immense periods of time' we can hear the waves slowly lapping at the edges of the Bassian Plain, and watch as grains of sand trickle slowly from sand dunes.

'Here be dragons: A view of Australian archaeology', in M.A. Smith, M. Spriggs and B. Fankhauser (eds.), *Sahul in Review: Pleistocene archaeology in Australia, New Guinea and Island Melanesia* (Canberra: Department of Prehistory, ANU, 1993), 11-16, 12.

JAMES HUTTON
On the geological record

(3-25) The result, therefore, of our present enquiry is, that we find no vestige of a beginning – no prospect of an end.

'Theory of the Earth', *Transactions of the Royal Society of Edinburgh* 1(2) (1788), 209-304, 304.

RHYS JONES
On the radiocarbon barrier

(3-26) Only in a few restricted areas of the continent … have we even got to the situation where simple questions as to the antiquity of human occupation and the main outlines of environmental change have been resolved … without taking cognizance of the ever dropping date for human occupation

of the continent, which like a falling trap door, is revealing
yawning depths beneath the false security of rope-bound
theories.

'Different strokes for different folks: Sites, Scale and Strategy', in I.
Johnson (ed.), *Holier than thou: Proceedings of the 1978 Kioloa conference on
Australian Prehistory* (Canberra: Department of Prehistory, ANU, 1980),
151-71, 153.

On the radio carbon revolution

(3-27) Radiocarbon dating however, acted to liberate
archaeologists from the shackles of the typological past and
in no other part of the world did the technique transform
the field more than it did in the Australian and Melanesian
theatres. ...a radical new technology of archaeological
investigation...

'A continental reconnaissance: some observations concerning the
discovery of the Pleistocene archaeology of Australia', in M. Spriggs (ed.),
A community of culture: the people and prehistory of the Pacific (Canberra:
Department of Prehistory, ANU, 1993), 97-122, 106, 108.

On the history of hunters

(3-28) In Tasmania, we have been able to document a record
of continuous human occupation as long as that which
separates the contemporary French farmer from the
Gravettian hunter who once stalked bison along the same
river flats, where rows of poplars now mark the boundaries
of meticulously tended fields.

'Hunting Forbears', in M. Roe (ed.), *The Flow of Culture: Tasmania studies*
(Canberra: Australian Academy of the Humanities, 1987), 14-49, 23.

NICHOLAS JOSE
On archaeological treasure

(3-29) Its real treasure was not gold or silver, but time itself ...

making palpable Australia's claim to be the oldest continent. There was a continuity between land and people that stretched further back than anywhere else. And the latest arrivals in Australia, immigrants all, wove themselves into the story as excavators and articulators.

A novelist's view, *The Custodians* (Sydney: Macmillan, 1997), 354.

RICHARD B. LEE AND IRVEN DEVORE
On the sustainability of a hunting and gathering way of life

(3-30) Of the estimated 80,000,000,000 men who have ever lived out a life span on earth, over 90 per cent have lived as hunters and gatherers; about 6 per cent have lived by agriculture and the remaining few per cent have lived in industrial societies. … It is still an open question whether man will be able to survive the exceedingly complex and unstable ecological conditions he has created for himself. If he fails in this task, interplanetary archeologists of the future will classify our planet as one in which a very long and stable period of small-scale hunting and gathering was followed by an apparently instantaneous efflorescence of technology and society leading rapidly to extinction. 'Stratigraphically,' the origin of agriculture and thermonuclear destruction will appear as essentially simultaneous.

'Problems in the study of hunters and gatherers', in R.B. Lee and I. Devore (eds.), *Man the Hunter* (Chicago: Aldine Pub. Co., 1968), 3-12, 3.

JOHN MCPHEE
On deep time

(3-31) Numbers do not seem to work well with regard to deep time. Any number above a couple of thousand years – fifty thousand, fifty million – will with nearly equal effect awe the imagination to the point of paralysis.

Annals of the Former World (New York: Farrar, Straus and Giroux, 1998), 29.

ANNE MICHAELS
On radiocarbon dating

(3-32) It's the moment of death we measure from.

Fugitive Pieces (New York: Vintage, 1998), 32.

On radioactivity and time

(3-33) It's no metaphor to feel the influence of the dead in the world, just as it's no metaphor to hear the radiocarbon chronometer, the Geiger counter amplifying the faint breathing of rock, fifty thousand years old.

Fugitive Pieces (New York: Vintage, 1998), 53.
[Editors' note: ^{14}C dating is not normally applied to rock, except perhaps carbonate minerals.]

JOHN MULVANEY
On the rapid advances in Australian archaeology in the 1960s

(3-34) No segment of the history of *Homo sapiens* had been so escalated since Darwin took time off the Mosaic standard.

'Archaeological Retrospect 9', *Antiquity* 60(229) (1986), 96-107, 102.

On the advent of radiocarbon dating

(3-35) A new time machine has been invented… Few readers will have heard of the 'carbon 14' method of dating the past, and those of who have may have dismissed it as scientific hocus-pocus. That this is not the case – that every intelligent layman should be acquainted with the results and realise their true implications – this brief survey hopes to demonstrate.

'A New Time Machine', *Twentieth Century* 8 (Spring 1952), 16-23, 16.

JOHN PLAYFAIR
On deep time

(3-36) ...the mind seemed to grow giddy by looking so far into the
abyss of time...

'Biographical Account of the Late Dr James Hutton, F.R.S. Edin.',
Transactions of the Royal Society of Edinburgh 5 (1805), 71-3, 73.

LYDIA V. PYNE AND STEPHEN J. PYNE
On measuring time

(3-37) Time is relative; it is measured by events as space is by
matter.

*The Last Lost World: Ice Ages, Human Origins, and the Invention of the
Pleistocene* (New York: Viking, 2012), 241.

RICHARD G. ROBERTS ET AL.
Beyond the radiocarbon barrier

(3-38) ...we are in the midst of a significant dating revolution.
With few extinct faunal successions, precise lithic
technologies and geomorphic benchmarks to guide us
at Australian sites, this process includes a diversification
of dating methods used in Australian archaeology. ...
Pleistocene chronologies should be constructed using the
widest range of appropriate dating techniques...

R.G. Roberts, R. Jones and M. Smith, 'Beyond the radiocarbon barrier in
Australian prehistory', *Antiquity* 68 (260) (1994), 611-16, 616.

WILLIAM SHAKESPEARE
Rosalind on the age of the earth

(3-39) ...the poor world is almost six thousand years old.

As You Like It, 4:1:83-4.

MIKE SMITH
On the glacial/interglacial sequence

(3-40) Cambridge scientists began to describe the deep-sea

sediments, as an 'orbital metronome'. Now one could imagine glacials and inter-glacials succeeding each other with each beat. Global climate now began to look precariously balanced. The earlier 1970s view was a primordial rather than processual view, an almost Biblical account of Ages. By the 1990s we seemed to be charting the oscillations of an unstable system.

'Palaeoclimates: An archaeology of climate change', in T. Sherrat, T. Griffiths and L. Robin (eds.), *A change in the weather: climate & culture in Australia* (Canberra: National Museum of Australia Press, 2005), 176-186, 178.

On a sense of place

(3-41) …we need not just a sense of place, but also a sense of place in time.

'Palaeoclimates: An archaeology of climate change', in T. Sherrat, T. Griffiths and L. Robin (eds.), *A change in the weather: climate & culture in Australia* (Canberra: National Museum of Australia Press, 2005), 176-186, 176.

W.E.H. (BILL) STANNER
On the Dreaming

(3-42) A central meaning of The Dreaming is that of a sacred, heroic time long ago when man and nature came to be as they are; but neither 'time' nor 'history' as we understand them is involved in this meaning. I have never been able to discover any Aboriginal word for *time* as an abstract concept. And the sense of 'history' is wholly alien here.

'The Dreaming' (1953), in *The Dreaming & Other Essays* (Melbourne: Black Inc. Agenda, 2009), 57.

(3-43) One cannot 'fix' The Dreaming in time: it was, and is everywhen,

'The Dreaming' (1953), in *The Dreaming & Other Essays* (Melbourne: Black Inc. Agenda, 2009), 58.

WALTER W. TAYLOR
On chronology as a means to an end

(3-44) Chronology is admittedly an important factor in any
archaeological research, and the easiest and surest method
of establishing it is to be commended. But after a sequence
of periods has been established, if then the very culture of
those periods is unknown, we may justifiably ask 'so what'?

'A Study of Archaeology', *Memoirs of The American Anthropological
Association* 69 (1948), 63.

DYLAN THOMAS
On time

(3-45) ...clocks with no hands for ever drumming out time
without ever knowing what time it is.

Under Milk Wood (London: Argo Record Co., 1954).

R.E.M. (MORTIMER) WHEELER
On chronology as a means to an end

(3-46) We must not allow chronology to monopolise our discipline.
It is a means to an end, not an end in itself.

Archaeology from the Earth (Oxford: Clarendon Press, 1954), 39.

ERIC WILMOT
On perception of time

(3-47) We as human beings, live in a flat time world, our total
reality is only an instant thick.

'The dragon principle', in Isabel McBryde (ed.), *Who Owns The Past*
(Melbourne: Oxford University Press, 1985), 41-48, 41.

4: ON SPACE, LANDSCAPES AND CLIMATE CHANGE

Climate and environmental change are key concerns of the field; but archaeological interest also extends to social landscapes, as these quotations illustrate.

R.J.C. (RICHARD) ATKINSON
On understanding a landscape

(4-1) ...half the business of field-work consists not in looking for sites, but in knowing where to look for them.

Field Archaeology (London: Methuen, 1946), 33.

JIM BOWLER
On the environmental archive represented by the Willandra lakes

(4-2) In their geomorphic and sedimentary features, these ancient lakes preserve in considerable detail the imprint of past changes in the physical environment to which they responded with particular sensitivity.

'Pleistocene salinities and climatic change: evidence from lakes and lunette in southeastern Australia', in D.J. Mulvaney and J. Golson (eds.), *Aboriginal Man and Environment in Australia* (Canberra: Australian National University Press, 1971), 47-65, 47.

WALLACE S. BROECKER
On the impact of human activities

(4-3) Climate is an ill-tempered beast, and we are poking it with sticks.

attrib. W.S. Broecker, cited in J. Adams, M. Maslin and E. Thomas, 'Sudden Climate Changes During the Quaternary', *Progress in Physical Geography* 23 (1999), 1-36, 29.

HAROLD C. BROOKFIELD
On landesque capital

(4-4) The innumerable stock-dams which dot the Australian landscape are landesque capital. Some landesque capital is so enduring that it can be re-used thousands of years after abandonment, given a new input of labour to get it back into working order, while other landesque capital has a much shorter life if not continuously maintained.

'Intensification Intensified,' *Archaeology in Oceania* 21 (3) (1986), 177-180, 179.

DIANA WOOD CONROY
On Lake Mungo

(4-5) A last marvellous walk on the lunette. It is a landscape at the end of its long life: the whole dune sequence eroding quickly, piling into white sand that flows to the east...

'Lake Mungo: Journeys between nature and culture', *A response to Lake Mungo: Long Gallery Faculty of Creative Arts, August 1-24, 1997* (Wollongong: University of Wollongong, 1997), 2-6, 2.

ROBERT L. CROCKER AND JOSEPH G. WOOD
On a postglacial period of severe aridity

(4-6) ...the Great Australian Arid Period...

'Some historical influences on the development of the South Australian vegetation communities and their bearing on concepts and classification in ecology', *Transactions of the Royal Society of South Australia* 71(1) (1947), 91-136, 118.

(4-7) The dessication was so severe and sudden that it resulted in a considerable portion of the pre-arid flora being entirely wiped out. The surviving remnants were isolated in numerous refuges... The present-day plant communities are the result of re-colonisation of vast, virtually bare, areas, especially in the arid regions.

'Some historical influences on the development of the South Australian vegetation communities and their bearing on concepts and classification in ecology', *Transactions of the Royal Society of South Australia* 71(1) (1947), 91-136, 129.

GREG DENING
On defining a landscape through language

(4-8) Language has filled the Land for millennia on millennia. Language brushes the land with metaphor. Language gives the most deserted place a history.

'Living in and with deep time' *Journal of Historical Sociology* 18(4) (2005), 269-281, 272.

KIRSTY DOUGLAS
On Lake Mungo

(4-9) The poster-child for human antiquity in Australia was, until twenty-five years ago, a working farm. 'Deep time' at Lake Mungo sits close to the surface, scoured out by wind and rain.

Pictures of time beneath: science, heritage and the uses of the deep past (Collingwood, VIC: CSIRO Publishing, 2010), 129.

WILLIAM J. DURANT
On the scale of geological change

(4-10) Civilization exists by geological consent, subject to change without notice.

attrib. W.J. Durant, 1926, in J.W. Rogers and T. Tucker, *Earth Science and Human History 101* (Westport, Conn Greenwood Press 2008), xiv.

JOHN FERRY
On the link between people and place in Aboriginal society
(4-11) The land was personalised, and the person was localised.

Colonial Armidale (St Lucia, QLD: University of Queensland Press, 1999), 2.

MILES FRANKLIN
On distance and perception
(4-12) But objects near the vision fill,

When one forgets the things afar;

A jam tin on the nearest hill

When touched by sunlight seems a star.

citing Bulletin verse, *The end of my career* (New York: Pocket Books, 1984), 146.

DAVID HORTON
On the last glacial maximum
(4-13) Australia is a continent on survival rations. ... If you thought Australia was a dry country in the late twentieth century, take a look at it now. This is the worst nightmare of Greenhouse theorists or El Nino analysts. This is dust blowing in your face and sand-dunes forming underfoot, and dry lakes and rivers that don't flow, and green is a colour you only see in dreams.

The Pure State of Nature: Sacred Cows, Destructive Myths and the Environment (St Leonards, NSW: Allen & Unwin, 2000), 111.

On the value of knowledge about the past
(4-14) As we face the Greenhouse Effect it is useful to know that the land has been both wetter and drier, and sea levels higher and lower, in the past.

'Here be dragons: A view of Australian archaeology', in M.A. Smith, M. Spriggs and B. Fankhauser (eds.), *Sahul in Review: Pleistocene archaeology in Australia, New Guinea and Island Melanesia* (Canberra: Department of Prehistory, ANU, 1993), 11-16, 15.

J.B. (BRINCK) JACKSON
On landscape as social order

(4-15) For the significance of space in landscape terms, the allotment of land for private or public use, is that it makes the social order visible.

The necessity for ruins (Amherst: University of Massachusetts Press, 1980), 115.

RHYS JONES
The antipodes through European eyes

(4-16) Palaeolithic or Neolithic; Hunter or Farmer; man a slave or master of his environment... Australia, the continent of hunters, and New Zealand, the islands of kumara and of pas, seem at first sight to symbolize this dichotomy, but the mediaeval schoolmen had always predicted that the antipodean world, when discovered, would be full of curiosities... Palaeolithic men using edge-ground axes? Farmers hunting giant birds? Fires moulding the landscape? It is indeed a strange world but who knows which is the obverse of which?

'The Neolithic, Palaeolithic and the hunting gardeners: man and land in the Antipodes', in R.P. Suggate and M. Cresswell (eds.), *Quaternary Studies* (Wellington: Royal Society of New Zealand, 1975), 21-34, 21.

On the meeting of two long-separated cultures

(4-17) The newcomers struggling through the surf were met on the beaches by other men looking at them from the edge of the trees. Thus the same landscape perceived by the newcomers as alien, hostile, or having no coherent form, was to the indigenous people their home, a familiar place, the inspiration of dreams.

'Ordering the Landscape', in I. Donaldson and T. Donaldson (eds.), *Seeing the First Australians* (Sydney: Allen & Unwin, 1985), 181-209, 185.

[Editors' note: This essay inspired the sculptural installation by Janet Laurence and Fiona Foley 'The Edge of the Trees' (1995) in the forecourt of the Museum of Sydney.]

On Canberra as a wilderness

(4-18) Here was a land empty of religious affiliation; there were no wells, no names of the totemic ancestors, no immutable links between land, people and the rest of the natural and supernatural worlds. Here was just a vast *tabula rasa*, cauterised of meaning… This land and its people therefore were analogous to the state of all the world once in some time before the Dreaming, before the great totemic Ancestral Beings strode across it, naming the places and giving it meaning. Viewed from this perspective, the Canberra of the geometric streets, and the paddocks of the six-wire fences were places not of domesticated order, but rather a wilderness of primordial chaos.

'Ordering the Landscape', in I. Donaldson and T. Donaldson (eds.), *Seeing the First Australians* (Sydney: Allen & Unwin, 1985), 181-209, 205-207.

On climate change

(4-19) Global Warming? Can't get enough.
Stoke it up higher.
Stop the next glaciation!
Save civilisation!

R. Jones, recorded by R. Williams, *The Science Show* (Australian Broadcasting Commission), 2001, published in 'A Tribute to Rhys Jones', *Australian Archaeology* 54 (2002), 59–60.

JOSEPH JOUBERT
On changing landscapes

(4-20) Places die, just as men do.

Cited in R. Depardon, M. Khemir, W. Thesiger and P. Virilio, *The Desert* (New York: Thames and Hudson, 2000), 102.

MARCIA LANGTON
On cultural landscapes

(4-21) Just as *terra nullius* was a lie, so was this European fantasy
of wilderness. There is no wilderness, but there are cultural
landscapes…

'Art, wilderness and *terra nullius*', in *Ecopolitics IX: Conference papers and
resolutions* (Darwin: Northern Land Council, 1996), 11-24, 24.

CHARLES F. LASERON
On landscape inheritance

(4-22) Beneath all – and here perhaps it is the geologist speaking
– is the evidence of a remote past. Nature is a tireless
sculpture, forever fashioning new masterpieces, yet, as if
unsatisfied commencing their destruction from the very
moment of their completion. Something of the old always
remains to be built into the new. The shape of a hill, the
contour of a waterfall, the rocky ledges on the sides of a
gully, the meanderings of a river, the alluvium of a plain
are all links with the past, and within them lies the story of
what has gone before.

'The Bush Around Us', in A.H. Chisholm, *Land of Wonder: The Best
Australian Nature Writing* (Sydney: Angus & Robertson, 1964), 30-31, 31.

PENELOPE LIVELY
On the world beneath the contemporary landscape

(4-23) You are looking at mayhem, all over Wiltshire and Dorset
and Somerset, those calm green counties with their
sleepy villages and cricket pitches and the primary school
playgrounds and the pubs with the hanging baskets that
drip petunias and lobelia. Surface veneer, all of it. Dig a few
feet and you are into blood-shed. The arrowheads and the

axes and the swords and the daggers. … This landscape is
howling, if you listen.

Making it up (New York: Viking, 2005), 78.

DAVID MALOUF
On the possibility of layered landscapes

(4-24) A land can bear any number of cultures laid one above
the other or set side by side. It can be inscribed and
written upon many times. One of those forms of writing
is the shaping of a landscape. In any place where humans
have made their home, the landscape will be a made one.
Landscape-making is in our bones.

A spirit of play: The making of Australian consciousness, Boyer Lectures 1998
(Sydney: ABC Books, 1998), 51.

HOWARD MORPHY
On landscape and the ancestral past

(4-25) The landscape is redolent with memories of other human
beings.

'Landscape and the Reproduction of the Ancestral Past', in E. Hirsch and
M. O'Hanlon (eds.), *The Anthropology of Landscape: Perspectives on Place
and Space* (Oxford: Clarendon, 1995), 184-209, 188.

FRED MYERS
On reading the landscape of the Pintupi people

(4-26) Had we the 'double vision' of poets, we could – perhaps
– read their history in the landscape itself, in the Gibson
Desert of Western Australia and the adjacent plateau of
central Australia to the east, at the edge of the magnificent
Macdonnell Ranges.

*Pintupi country, Pintupi self: sentiment, place, and politics among western
desert Aborigines* (Canberra: Australian Institute of Aboriginal Studies,
1986) 11.

MICHAEL J. ROWLAND
On landscape and environment as agency

(4-27) Space is not just a raw material to be shaped by social process, and landscapes are not merely symbolic constructs. People in the past, as they do today, responded directly to environmental changes, but also indirectly to changes in landscape and resource distribution that were initiated by the changes.

'Holocene Environmental Variability: Have its Impacts Been Underestimated in Australian Pre History?', *The Artefact* 22 (1999), 11-40, 12.

SIMON SCHAMA
On the cultural construction of landscape

(4-28) ...landscapes are culture before they are nature; constructs of the imagination projected onto wood and water and rock.

Landscape and Memory (New York: Vintage Books, 1996), 61.

GEORGE SEDDON
On the importance of landscape

(4-29) Human history is not complete without environmental history. It is not enough to detail the actions of the actors; the stage is equally important.

'Thinking like a geologist: The culture of geology', Mawson Lecture, *Australian Journal of Earth Sciences* 43 (1996), 487-95, 495.

J.M.B. (JEREMY) SMITH
On the dynamics of vegetation

(4-30) Vegetation is vibrant with change – with short-term fluctuations, medium-term successions and longer-term evolutionary changes; its constituent taxa are ever able to migrate wherever conditions in some way change to allow it.

'An Introduction to the History of the Australasian Vegetation', in J.M.B. Smith (ed.), *A history of Australasian vegetation* (Sydney: McGraw-Hill, 1982), 1-31, 27.

MIKE SMITH
On the desert landscape as a historical document

(4-31) …I think of these landscapes as a palimpsest of different deserts, stratified in time, stacked one above another, each with its climates, physical landscapes and environments; each with its social landscapes and people, places of association and belonging, territories, resources, and itineraries. Some features of earlier deserts project through and become part of the fabric and cultural geography of later deserts. Some structural features and processes are held in common: wind and water shape landforms; the basin and range topography provides the form of the landscape. No one desert is entirely erased by succeeding deserts – a fact that makes archaeology possible. Whatever else it may be, a desert landscape is a historical document preserving a complex record of the interaction of past climates, environments, and cultural systems.

'Reading Puritjarra', in M. Martin, L. Robin and M.A. Smith (eds.), *Strata: Deserts past, present and future* (Mandurama, NSW: Mandy Martin, 2005), 19-24, 20.

On changes in palaeo-environment

(4-32) Two great processes dominate the Quaternary history of Australia: the expansion of the deserts, and the rise of the sea. Between the two lie the temperate fertile crescents of south-western and south-eastern Australia. In response to these changes, the archaeological record preserves a regional

history of re-organisation of settlement, repositioning
of cultural landscapes, small-scale movement of people
in response to the changing configuration of resources,
changes in trade routes and possibly religious networks, and
in regional economies.

'Palaeoclimates: An archaeology of climate change', in T. Sherrat, T.
Griffiths and L. Robin (eds.), *A change in the weather: climate & culture
in Australia* (Canberra: National Museum of Australia Press, 2005),
176-186, 180.

On Millennial Megaflickers

(4-33) You need to remember that only 5-6°C separates our
climate today from that at the height of the last Ice Age.
Minus 5°C will see an alpine meadow with button grass
transformed into a wilderness of ice and cold, slowly
being ground into rock flour under the weight of several
kilometres of ice. ... How much climate change is required
to transform the bed of Lake Mungo from a world of
waterfowl, perch and crayfish to one of saltbush, red
kangaroo and emu?

'Palaeoclimates: An archaeology of climate change', in T. Sherrat, T.
Griffiths and L. Robin (eds.), *A change in the weather: climate & culture
in Australia* (Canberra: National Museum of Australia Press, 2005),
176-186, 178.

On the fugitive traces of hunter-gatherer societies

(4-34) ...hunter gatherer societies tend to be 'soft shelled' and
leave little fossil imprint. ... Australian archaeologists have
to work with a very coarse-grained historical geography.
Our archaeological sequences bear witness to the birth and
death of cultural landscapes rather than the finer-grained
pulse of cultural ecology.

'Palaeoclimates: An archaeology of climate change', in T. Sherrat, T.
Griffiths and L. Robin (eds.), *A change in the weather: climate & culture in*

Australia (Canberra: National Museum of Australia Press, 2005), 176-186, 185-6.

RALPH TATE
On increased rainfall in the interior of Australia in the past

(4-35) A vastly increased rainfall over what is now the arid region of Australia in former times is demanded by the extinct rivers and lakes and the former existence of large herbivores … a glacial period and a pluvial period mean the same to me.

'Post-Miocene climate in South Australia', *Transactions and Proceedings and Report of the Royal Society of South Australia 8 (1886)*, 49-59, 53.

On the expectation of montane refugia

(4-36) I had pictured a vast mountain system capable of preserving some remnants of that pristine flora which had existed on this continent in Palaeocene times – probably a beech, possibly an oak, elm or sycamore.

'Botany', in B. Spencer (ed.), *Report on the work of the Horn scientific expedition to Central Australia, Part III: Geology and Botany* (London: Dulau, 1896), 117-94, 118.

YI-FU TUAN
On creation of a cultural landscape

(4-37) What begins as undifferentiated space becomes place as we get to know it better and endow it with value.

Space and place: the perspective of experience (London: Edward Arnold, 1977), 6.

DONALD WALKER
On climatic explanations

(4-38) …it is all too easy to become like a child with Christmas chocolates. We open the box of Climatic Assorteds and take our pick of the seductive dainties inside: frosted springs, misty mornings, hot noons, or even glacier mints! Sometimes, with true experimental dash we try something just because we have not tried it before.

'Limitations of Some Biological Bases of Palaeoclimatology', *Australian Meteorological Magazine* 24(1) (1976), 21-32, 23.

CHARLES S. WILKINSON
On the Cuddie Springs fossil site

(4-39) ...nothing but want of water could have brought together such a heterogeneous assemblage of animals to the same drinking place; and what must have been their last terrible struggle for existence, as the supply of water failed, must be beyond description.

'President's Address', *Proceedings of the Linnean Society of New South Wales* 9 (1885), 1207-41, 1238.

JOHN WOLSELEY
On a layered landscape

(4-40) We pay too much attention to the surface of the earth – it presents itself so obviously to our eyes. We forget the layers above and below – the interweaving lines which connect paths of energy and moving particles – and the traces of long past events: flying spiders, slowly moving clouds of pollen, flight paths of birds and the tunnels of blind insects.

Quoted in S. Grishin, *John Wolseley: Land Marks* (Fishermans Bend, VIC: Craftsman House, 1998), 145.

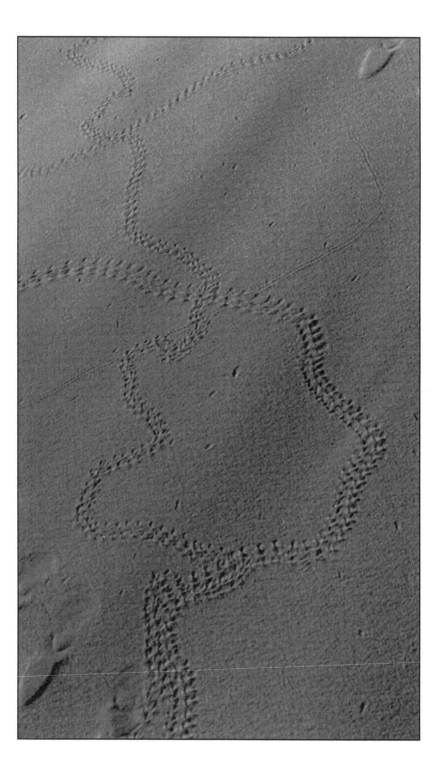

5: ON DESERTS IN PARTICULAR

Australia is the 'desert continent'. These quotations reflect on a special type of landscape for archaeologists, and a dynamic field of research.

ANON
On dying of thirst

(5-1) …my tung is stiking to my mouth and I see what I have rote and know this is the last time I may have of expressing feeling. Blind … for want of water. My ey Dazels my tong burn. I can see no way. God help.

Last words scratched on a billy can by a dying shepherd, near Lake Torrens, 1858, attrib. to Billy Colter, cited in R.G. Kimber, *Man from Arltunga: Walter Smith, Australian Bushman* (Alice Springs: Hesperian Press, 1986), 28.

EDWARD ABBEY
On the austerity of the desert

(5-2) The desert says nothing. Completely passive, acted upon but never acting, the desert lies there like the bare skeleton of Being, spare, sparse, austere, utterly worthless, inviting not love but contemplation. … Motionless and silent it evokes in us an elusive hint of something unknown, unknowable, about to be revealed. Since the desert does not act it seems to be waiting – but waiting for what?

Desert Solitaire (Tucson: University of Arizona Press, 1988), 210.

RALPH BAGNOLD
On sand dunes

(5-3) Here, instead of finding chaos and disorder, the observer never fails to be amazed at a simplicity of form, an exactitude of repetition and a geometric order unknown in nature on a scale larger than that of crystalline structure. In places vast accumulations of sand weighing millions of tons move inexorably, in regular formation, over the surface of the country, growing, retaining their shape, even breeding, in a manner which, by its grotesque imitation of life, is vaguely disturbing to an imaginative mind.

The physics of blown sand and desert dunes (New York: William Morrow, 1941), xxi.

ISAIAH BOWMAN
On the diversity of deserts

(5-4) Deserts are no more alike than mountains or plains.

Desert trails of Atacama (New York, American Geographical Society, 1924), 60.

GEORGE DANIEL BROCK
On hopes for an inland sea

(5-5) The Captain feels dreadfully chagrined that the lake is *dry* – the most sanguine hopes have been entertained that we should float the boat on Lake Torrens, but there is barely water to float a duck.

To the desert with Sturt: A diary of the 1844 expedition (Adelaide: SA Government Printer, 1988), 171-2.

SCOTT CANE
On desert subsistence

(5-6) The size and number of the major waterholes control foraging movement. Water shortages and heat stress prevent people from traveling to areas where food is still available and, in a sense, people become trapped on foraging 'islands' around large waterholes.

'Australian Aboriginal Subsistence in the Western Desert', *Human Ecology* 15 (1987), 391-434, 395.

On completing first-order exploration of the continent

(5-7) We've found 'the corners of the room', but is it 'a room with
a view'?

Unpublished comment, Australian National University, 1990.

On the notion of glacial refugia

(5-8) Each desert has its own barriers, corridors and refuges
and one should look to this inner variability in order to
understand the true nature of desert colonisation and
settlement. A position of graduated marginality may be a
better way of describing the desert lands...

*Nullarbor antiquity: Archaeological, luminescent and seismic investigations on
the Nullarbor Plain* (Port Lincoln, SA: Culture and Heritage, 1995), 49.

DAVID W. CARNEGIE
On the Great Sandy Desert

(5-9) A vast, howling wilderness of high, spinifex-clad ridges of
red sand, so close together that in a day's march we crossed
from sixty to eighty ridges, so steep that often the camels
had to crest them on their knees, and so barren and destitute
of vegetation (saving spinifex) that one marvels how even
camels could pick up a living.

Spinifex and Sand (Victoria Park, WA: Hesperian Press, 1982), 249-50.

DEUTERONOMY

(5-10) In a desert land ... in a barren and howling waste.

Deuteronomy 32:10, *New International Version.*

H.H. (HEDLEY) FINLAYSON
On dying of thirst

(5-11) 'To perish,' is to die by weathering, and like gutta-percha,

men lose elasticity in the change, and the end product is
known far and wide as a 'stiff un.'

The red centre: man and beast in the heart of Australia (Sydney: Angus &
Robertson, 1935), 145.

On the Red Centre

(5-12) The drabness which characterizes the more southerly dry
country – the greys and dull greens, the fawns and faded
browns of the saltbush tablelands, for example – have little
place here; and it might well be known as the Red Centre.
Sand, soil, and most of the rocks are a fiery cinnabar...

The red centre: man and beast in the heart of Australia (Sydney: Angus &
Robertson, 1935), 22.

ERNEST GILES
On being stranded in the Gibson Desert

(5-13) I became so thirsty at each step I took that I longed to drink
up every drop of water I had in the keg, but it was the elixir
of death I was burdened with, and to drink it was to die.

Australia Twice Traversed, vol. 2 (London: S. Low, Marston, Searle &
Rivington, Limited, 1889), 39.

RICHARD A. GOULD
On 'the loneliest place on earth'

(5-14) ...the Aborigines living on the mission today speak of the
desert where they once lived as being 'too lonely'... Today
the Gibson Desert is the loneliest place on earth, lonelier
even than the wastes of Antarctica. What can be lonelier
than a place where people have lived their lives and then left
forever?

Yiwara: Foragers of the Australian Desert (New York: Scribner, 1969), 167, 192.

On prehistoric desert adaptation

(5-15) Although some changes are evident in the stone toolkit, these are outweighed by evidence for cultural continuities pointing to a relatively stable adaptation to rigorous post-Pleistocene conditions in the Western Desert which has continued to the present. ... This adaptive model is termed the Australian desert culture.

'Puntutjarpa Rockshelter and the Australian desert culture',
Anthropological Papers of the American Museum of Natural History 54(1)
(1977), 1-187, 5.

On the desert as a leveller of ambition

(5-16) From a deterministic viewpoint, the core desert can be seen as a great leveller of human behaviour in the sense that it limits the optional responses by anyone with a hunting-and-gathering mode of subsistence who tries to live there. ...anyone attempting to follow a seasonal round or adapt in any other way would undoubtedly perish.

'Puntutjarpa Rockshelter and the Australian desert culture',
Anthropological Papers of the American Museum of Natural History 54(1)
(1977), 1-187, 182.

On desert conservatism

(5-17) The cultural sequence at Puntutjarpa Rockshelter thus provides evidence for the success of this ancient desert culture adaptation throughout the post-Pleistocene of the Western Desert, culminating in the ethnographic desert culture of that region, in what must surely stand as one of the most dramatic cases of cultural conservatism on record.

'Puntutjarpa Rockshelter and the Australian desert culture',
Anthropological Papers of the American Museum of Natural History 54(1)
(1977), 1-187, 182.

J.W. (JOHN) GREGORY
The arid core of the continent

(5-18) The Dead Heart of Australia

> Book title, *The Dead Heart of Australia: A Journey around Lake Eyre in the Summer of 1901-1902, with some account of the Lake Eyre basin and the flowing wells of Central Australia* (London: John Murray, 1906).

On the development of aridity in the Lake Eyre basin

(5-19) The rainfall dwindled, the water-level sank, and the lake decreased in size. …the waters became salt and the fish and crocodiles were all destroyed. …the giant marsupials died of hunger and thirst; hot winds swept across the dusty plains, and the once fertile basin of Lake Eyre was blasted into desert.

> *The Dead Heart of Australia: A Journey around Lake Eyre in the Summer of 1901-1902, with some account of the Lake Eyre basin and the flowing wells of Central Australia* (London: John Murray, 1906), 151.

PETER HISCOCK AND LYNLEY WALLIS
On settlement of the desert interior during a mesic phase

(5-20) This 'desert transformation' model removes the paradox of explaining how people were able to migrate into Australian deserts in the late Pleistocene; in some important ways the modern deserts of Australia came to inland dwelling people, rather than the reverse.

> 'Pleistocene settlement of deserts from an Australian perspective', in P. Veth, M. Smith and P. Hiscock (eds.), *Desert peoples: archaeological perspectives* (Oxford: Blackwell, 2005), 42.

PETER HISCOCK AND PETER VETH
On a dynamic prehistory

(5-21) The notion of the conservative Australian Desert Culture is no longer tenable.

> 'Change in the Australian desert culture: A reanalysis of tulas from Puntutjarpa rockshelter', *World Archaeology* 22(3) (1991), 332-345, 343.

RHYS JONES
On occupation of the desert

(5-22) Paradoxically, having mastered the capacity to cross water, the true barrier to the colonization of the Australian continent lay not in the occupation of the tropical north but in the extension south into the dry regions of the continent.

'Pleistocene life in the dead heart of Australia', *Nature* 328 (1987), 666.

HENRY LAWSON
On Australia

(5-23) 'Good country!' exclaimed the man with the grey beard, in a tone of disgust. 'Why, it's only a mongrel desert, except some bits round the coast. The worst dried-up and God-forsaken country I was ever in.'

'His Country – After All', in H. Lawson, *While the Billy Boils* (Sydney: Angus and Robertson, 1896), 40.

IMANUEL NOY-MEIR
Definition of a desert

(5-24) Let us now ignore the exceptions and define desert ecosystems as 'water-controlled ecosystems with infrequent, discrete and largely unpredictable water inputs.'

'Desert ecosystems: environment and producers,' *Annual Review of Ecology and Systematic* 4 (1973), 25-51, 26.

MARK O'CONNOR
On the great dune fields of arid Australia

(5-25) The sand with its slow-motion breakers
is the inland sea, that spills
over half a continent, its tides
swirling in millennial time
through archipelagos of red-earth hills

with here and there blue shadows of forest
floating like seawrack.

'Dot Paintings', in *The Olive Tree: collected poems 1972-2000* (Sydney: Hale
& Iremonger, 2000), 229.

SUE O'CONNOR AND PETER VETH
On the arid Kimberley coast

(5-26) Where the Desert Meets the Sea…

Title of an article, 'Where the Desert Meets the Sea: A Preliminary
Report of the Archaeology of the Southern Kimberley Coast', *Australian
Archaeology* 37 (1993), 25-34.

LIBBY ROBIN
On the critical role of resource-rich patches in desert ecology

(5-27) Detail is the new 'big picture'.

In L. Robin and M. Smith, 'Science in place and time', in C. Dickman,
D. Lunney and S. Burgin (eds.), *Animals of Arid Australia: out on their
own?* (Sydney: Royal Zoological Society of New South Wales, 2007),
188-196, 191.

ANTOINE DE SAINT-EXUPÉRY
On the Sahara

(5-28) Life here evaporates like a vapor. Bedouins, explorers, and
colonial officers all tell us that a man may go nineteen hours
without water. Thereafter his eyes fill with light, and that
marks the beginning of the end. The progress made by thirst
is swift and terrible.

Wind, Sand and Stars, transl. by L. Galantière (London: The Folio Society,
1990), 135.

(5-29) I have always loved the desert. One sits down on a desert
sand dune, sees nothing, hears nothing. Yet through the
silence something throbs, and gleams…

The Little Prince, transl. by K. Woods (New York: Trumpet club, 1988), 92.

PERCY BYSSHE SHELLEY
On deserts as a metaphor for the impermanence of power

(5-30) I met a traveller from an antique land
　　　Who said: Two vast and trunkless legs of stone
　　　Stand in the desert. Near them, on the sand,
　　　Half sunk, a shattered visage lies, whose frown,
　　　And wrinkled lip, and sneer of cold command,
　　　Tell that its sculptor well those passions read
　　　Which yet survive, stamped on these lifeless things,
　　　The hand that mocked them and the heart that fed:
　　　And on the pedestal these words appear:
　　　'My name is Ozymandias, king of kings:
　　　Look on my works, ye Mighty, and despair!'
　　　Nothing beside remains. Round the decay
　　　Of that colossal wreck, boundless and bare
　　　The lone and level sands stretch far away.

'Ozymandias' (1819), in *The poetical works of Percy Bysshe Shelley* (London: Frederick Warne, 1888), 553.

MIKE SMITH
On a more dynamic prehistory

(5-31) The notion of a stable *desert culture* now seems obsolete.

The pattern and timing of prehistoric settlement in Central Australia, PhD thesis, University of New England, 1988, 343.

On wells as stepping stones

(5-32) …unlike the coast, the human history of the desert
　　　is more a story of critical resources than transformed
　　　landscapes: a history of water with a small 'w'. It is the
　　　fluctuating fortunes of wells and soakages, claypan waters
　　　and ephemeral lakes that determine access to the country
　　　for foragers. These waters are stepping stones through the
　　　country. Remove them and access to country and its sparse

resources is more limited, the living space of hunters and foragers more confined.

'Palaeoclimates: An archaeology of climate change', in T. Sherrat, T. Griffiths and L. Robin (eds.), *A change in the weather: climate & culture in Australia* (Canberra: National Museum of Australia Press, 2005), 176-186, 182.

On the boom and bust ecology of Australia's deserts

(5-33) …deserts are characterised not just by scarcity but also by transient richness. … In some respects, the desert is an unstable extension of the savanna, shrublands and grasslands surrounding the region.

The archaeology of Australia's deserts (Cambridge: Cambridge University Press, 2013), 8.

CHARLES STURT
On entering the Simpson dunefield

(5-34) Ascending one of the sand ridges I saw a numberless succession of these terrific objects rising above each other to the east and west of me. Northwards they ran away before me for more than fifteen miles, with the most undeviating straightness, as if those masses had been thrown up with the plumb and rule. How much farther they went with the same undeviating regularity God only knows. … The scene was awfully fearful, dear Charlotte. A kind of dread … came over me as I gazed upon it. It looked like the entrance into Hell.

Journal of the Central Australian Expedition 1844-1845 (London: Caliban Books, 1984), 72-74.

GRIFFITH TAYLOR
On describing the arid interior

(5-35) There was universal objection to using the term 'desert' for any part of the Australian interior. I imagine that Australians now realise that a desert by any other name is just as dry.

'Australia's barren spaces', *Sydney Morning Herald*, 16 December 1944, 8.

PETER VETH
On glacial refugia as adaptive filters

(5-36) The colonisers of interior Australia would only have become pre-adapted to truly arid conditions within the refuges of the glacial maximum, the islands of the interior.

Islands in the interior: the dynamics of prehistoric adaptations within the Arid Zone of Australia (Ann Arbor: International Monographs in Prehistory, 1993), 114.

PETER EGERTON WARBURTON
On crossing the Great Sandy Desert

(5-37) Our journey has been a very hard one, and we have suffered great privations; but they could not have been guarded against, because we did not know the nature of the country we had to cross.

Journey across the western interior of Australia (Victoria Park, WA: Hesperian Press, 1981), 294.

FRED WILLIAMS
An artist's impression of a desert landscape

(5-38) To see the desert is like peeling the skin off a landscape.

Quoted in S. McGrath and J. Olsen, *The artist and the desert* (Sydney: Bay Books, 1981), 110.

6: ON ABORIGINAL SOCIETY AND THE DREAMING

Australian archaeology is concerned with reconstructing the deep history of Aboriginal society. So archaeologists need to be cultural scholars as well as dispassionate scientists. This eclectic selection of quotations – penned mainly by scholars outside the field – reflects changing perceptions of Aboriginal societies over time.

ANON
A desert people's view on meetings

(6-1) palilpa n. (Pintupi/Luritja) lit. 'Tiredness of spirit – resulting from continually attending meetings.'

K.C. Hansen and L.E. Hansen (eds.), *Pintupi/Luritja dictionary* (Alice Springs: Institute for Aboriginal Development, 1977), 92.

RONALD M. BERNDT
On initiation into a totemic geography

(6-2) The whole religious corpus vibrated with an expressed aspiration for life, abundant life. Vitality, fertility and growth... Initiation for males, particularly, really served as an introduction to a new discipline, an expansive and expanding area of knowledge, a new way of looking at things within the social, natural and supernatural environments.

Australian Aboriginal religion (Leiden: Brill, 1974), 4.

On Palaeolithic survivals

(6-3) ...these Aborigines were not a 'Stone Age' people or Palaeolithic survivals; nor were their culture and social organisation.

Australian Aboriginal religion (Leiden: Brill, 1974), 4.

EDMUND BURKE
On the notion that social evolution can be traced in contemporary societies

(6-4) …we possess at this time very great advantages towards the knowledge of human Nature. We need no longer go to History to trace it in all its stages and periods. … But now the Great Map of Mankind is unrolld at once; and there is no state or Graduation of barbarism, and no mode of refinement which we have not at the same instant under our View.

E. Burke to W. Robertson, 9 June 1777, in *Selected Letters of Edmund Burke* (Chicago: The University of Chicago Press, 1984), 102.

BRUCE CHATWIN
On dreaming tracks and mythological trails

(6-5) I have a vision of the Songlines stretching across the continents and ages; that wherever men have trodden they have left a trail of song (of which we may, now and then, catch an echo); and that these trails must reach back, in time and space, to an isolated pocket in the African savannah…

Songlines (London: Picador, 1988), 280.

ALFRED W. CROSBY
On the technological and economic gap

(6-6) When Captain Cook and the Australians of Botany Bay looked at each other in the eighteenth century, they did so from opposite sides of the Neolithic Revolution.

Ecological Imperialism: The biological expansion of Europe 900-1900 (Cambridge: Cambridge University Press, 1986), 18.

JOHN DRYDEN
On the noble savage

(6-7) I am as free as nature first made man,
   Ere the base laws of servitude began,
   When wild in woods the noble savage ran.

Almanzor, in *The Conquest of Granada by the Spaniards* (In the Savoy: Printed by T.N. for Henry Herringman, 1672), 7.

EDWARD JOHN EYRE
On developing Aboriginal history

(6-8) The continent of Australia is so vast, and the dialects, customs, and ceremonies of its inhabitants so varied in detail, though so similar in general outline and character, that it will require the lapse of years, and the labours of many individuals, to detect and exhibit the links which form the chain of connection in the habits and history of tribes so remotely separated; and it will be long before any one can attempt to give to the world a complete and well-drawn outline of the whole.

Journals of Expeditions of Discovery into Central Australia, and Overland from Adelaide to King George's Sound, in the years 1840-1,-vol. 2 (London: T. and W. Boone, 1845), 152.

MARTIN GIBBS AND PETER VETH
On the spread of Western Desert societies

(6-9) ...the remarkable geographic spread and speed of transmission was driven by a set of social imperatives that we will characterise here as 'ritual engines'.

'Ritual engines and the archaeology of territorial ascendancy', *Tempus* 7 (2002), 11-19, 11.

FRANK GILLEN
On a storied landscape

(6-10) ...there is not a remarkable natural feature in the country without a special tradition – tradition – why it is the very breath of their nostrils...

Gillen, letter to Baldwin Spencer, cited in D.J. Mulvaney and J. Calaby, *So much that is new: Baldwin Spencer 1860-1929, A biography* (Carlton, VIC: University of Melbourne, 1985), 177.

DAN GILLESPIE
On the ecological *savoir-faire* of Aboriginal people

(6-11) Aboriginal people understand ecosystems like other people wear old overcoats. They know where the thin bits are and know how far they can stretch them before they tear.

Comment at seminar, Australian National University, 1988.

RICHARD A. GOULD
On the Dreaming

(6-12) Gradually I experienced the central truth of Aboriginal religion: that it is not a thing by itself but an inseparable part of a whole that encompasses every aspect of daily life, every individual, and every time – past, present, and future. It is nothing less than the theme of existence, and as such constitutes one of the most sophisticated and unique religious and philosophical systems known to man.

Yiwara: Foragers of the Australian Desert (New York: Scribner, 1969), 103-104.

THOMAS HOBBES
On primitive society

(6-13) No arts; no letters; no society; and which is worst of all, continual fear, and danger of violent death: and the life of man, solitary, poor, nasty, brutish and short.

Leviathan, pt. 1, ch. 13 (1651).

PHILIP JONES
On red ochre

(6-14) …red ochre is a medium or agent of transcendence, from
sickness to health, death to renewal, ritual uncleanness to
cleanness, the secular to the sacred, the present reality to the
Dreaming.

Ochre and Rust: Artefacts and Encounters on Australian Frontiers (Kent
Town, SA: Wakefield Press, 2007), 349.

RHYS JONES
On the economic cost of great ceremonies

(6-15) The economic consequences of the great ceremonies have
however been less stressed, perhaps because so few have
been observed, whose logistic support came from foraged
food. In 1972-73 the Gidjingali organised amongst minor
rituals, two major *Kunapipi* ceremonies, whose climaxes
brought together two to 300 people. An investment of some
400 man weeks was made in carrying these out. Elsewhere,
I have shown that this much labour might have erected
a small hill fort, cleared many acres of ground or written
two and a half Ph.D theses, had these been the aims of the
society.

'The Tasmanian Paradox', in R.V.S. Wright (ed.), *Stone Tools as Cultural
Markers: change, evolution and complexity* (Canberra: Australian Institute
of Aboriginal Studies, 1977), 189-204, 201.

On hunters and history

(6-16) Yet contemporary hunters are not static relics from a frozen
past; they also have their own past that can be investigated
archaeologically.

'Hunters and history: A case study from western Tasmania', in C. Schrire
(ed.), *Past and Present in Hunter Gatherer Studies* (London: Academic
Press, 1984), 27-65, 59.

JOHN KING
On chewing the narcotic *pituri*

(6-17) …after chewing it for a few minutes I felt quite happy and perfectly indifferent about my position.

The sole survivor of the Burke and Wills expedition, cited in A. Moorehead, *Cooper's Creek: The real story of Burke and Wills* (South Melbourne: Sun Books, 1985), 118.

CLAUDE LÉVI-STRAUSS
On the cultural complexity of Aboriginal societies

(6-18) …few civilizations seem to equal the Australians in their taste for erudition and speculation and what sometimes looks like intellectual dandyism, odd as this expression may appear when it is applied to people with so rudimentary a level of material life.

The Savage Mind, transl. by anon (London: Weidenfeld and Nicholson, 1966), 89.

On the concept of primitiveness

(6-19) I see no reason why mankind should have waited until recent times to produce minds of the calibre of a Plato or an Einstein. Already over two or three hundred thousand years ago, there were probably men of a similar capacity…

'The concept of primitiveness', in R.B. Lee and I. Devore (eds.), *Man the Hunter* (Chicago: Aldine Pub. Co., 1968), 349-352, 351.

BETTY MEEHAN
On dinnertime camps

(6-20) 'Dinnertime camps' … are small camp sites used during the middle of the day while people are engaged in hunting trips away from their home base.

Shell Bed to Shell Midden (Canberra: Australian Institute of Aboriginal Studies, 1982), 26.

HOWARD MORPHY
On a totemic geography

(6-21) Art provides a sacred charter to the land...

Aboriginal Art (London: Phaidon Press, 1998), 5.

JOHN MULVANEY
On the dynamic nature of Aboriginal society

(6-22) Aboriginal society, despite its latter-day critics, was never static. There was scope for the innovator as well as for the dreamer, and the Aborigines were not captives of an unchanging and hostile environment. That is the essence of Aboriginal prehistory, which endows it with the creativity of the human spirit.

Concluding words, *The Prehistory of Australia* (Ringwood, VIC: Penguin Books, 1975), 282.

On the spiritual life of Aboriginal people

(6-23) Before posing the 'why no neolithic?' question, therefore, it must be observed that an Aboriginal was possibly healthier than a peasant in classical Rome and better adjusted than a New York apartment dweller. Pharoah's pyramid testifies to his society's technological mastery, but it perished; archaeology hints at an extraordinary continuity of social adjustment and spiritual life within Australia.

The Prehistory of Australia (Ringwood, VIC: Penguin Books, 1975), 239.

On long distance trade and exchange

(6-24) In theory, it was possible for a man who had brought pituri from the Mulligan River and ochre from Parachilna to own a Cloncurry axe, a Boulia boomerang and wear shell pendants from Carpentaria and Kimberley.

'"The chain of connection": The material evidence', in N. Peterson (ed.), *Tribes and boundaries in Australia* (Canberra: Australian Institute of Aboriginal Studies, 1976), 72-94, 80.

FRED MYERS
On land tenure

(6-25) …'holding country' primarily consists in control over the
stories, objects, and rituals associated with the mythological
ancestors of the Dreaming at a particular place.

'Place, identity, and exchange in a totemic system: Nurturance and
the process of social reproduction in Pintupi society', in J. Fajans (ed.),
Exchanging products: Producing exchange (Sydney: University of Sydney,
1993), 33-57, 45.

BILL NEIDJIE
On historicising the Dreaming

(6-26) Our story is in the land…
it is written in those sacred places.
My children will look after those places,
that's the law.

…

When that law started?
I don't know how many thousand years.
European say 40,000 years,
but I reckon myself probably was more because…
it is sacred.

B. Neidjie, S. Davis and A. Fox, *Kakadu man…Bill Neidjie* (Darwin:
Mybrood, 1986), 47-48.

NICOLAS PETERSON
On Aboriginal society

(6-27) …the problem is that the Australian's elementary forms
of religious and social life are nothing like as elementary
as once thought: indeed, one well-known anthropologist
remarked at a recent conference that Durkheim should

have written about the people he worked with for really
elementary forms.

'Comments and Reply', in A. Testart, 'Some major problems in the social
anthropology of hunter-gatherers', *Current Anthropology* 29(1) (1988),
1-31, 20.

NICOLAS PETERSON AND JEREMY LONG
On inclusion in desert society

(6-28) At the desert end of the continuum descent is a metaphor
manifested in such phrases as, 'my father's country' as an
explanation or claim. … Because the population density
is so low, groups are small, sociability is stretched to its
uttermost and the emphasis is on inclusion.

Australian territorial organization: a band perspective (Sydney: University of
Sydney, 1986), 151-2.

DEBORAH BIRD ROSE
On country as 'nourishing terrain'

(6-29) People talk about country in the same way that they would
talk about a person: they speak to country, sing to country,
visit country, worry about country, feel sorry for country
and long for country … country knows, hears, smells, takes
notice, takes care, is sorry or happy… Because of this
richness, country is home, and peace; nourishment for body,
mind and spirit; heart's ease.

*Nourishing Terrain: Australian Aboriginal Views of Landscape and
Wilderness* (Canberra: Australian Heritage Division, 1996), 7.

MARSHALL SAHLINS
On the hunter-gatherer way of life

(6-30) …this was, when you come to think of it, the original
affluent society.

'Notes on the original affluent society', in R.B. Lee and I. Devore (eds.),
Man the Hunter (Chicago: Aldine Pub. Co., 1968), 85-89, 85.

WILLIAM J. SOLLAS
On 'living fossils'

(6-31) To commence a chapter on Pleistocene man by an account
of a recent race might well seem a wilful anachronism;
the Tasmanians, however, though recent, were at the same
time a Palaeolithic or even, it has been rashly asserted, an
Eolithic race; and they thus afford us an opportunity of
interpreting the past by the present – a saving procedure
in a subject where fantasy is only too likely to play a
leading part. We will therefore first direct our attention
to the habits and mode of life of this isolated people, the
most unprogressive in the world, which in the middle of
the nineteenth century was still living in the dawn of the
Palaeolithic epoch.

Ancient Hunters and Their Modern Representatives (London: Macmillan
and co., limited, 1911), 87.

BALDWIN SPENCER AND FRANK GILLEN
On the evolutionary position of Aboriginal people

(6-32) Australia is the present home and refuge of creatures,
often crude and quaint, that have elsewhere passed away
and given place to higher forms. This applies equally to
the aboriginal as to the platypus and kangaroo. Just as
the platypus, laying its eggs and feebly suckling its young,
reveals a mammal in the making, so does the Aboriginal
show us, at least in broad outline, what early man must have
been like before he learned to read and write, domesticate
animals, cultivate crops, and use a metal tool. It has been
possible to study in Australia human beings that still remain
on the cultural level of men of the Stone Age.

The Arunta: a study of a stone age people (London: Macmillan and co.,
1927), vii.

W.E.H. (BILL) STANNER
On the Dreaming

(6-33) Clearly, The Dreaming is many things in one. Among them, a kind of narrative to things that once happened; a kind of charter of things that still happen; and a kind of *logos* or principle of order transcending everything significant for Aboriginal man.

'The Dreaming' (1953), in *The Dreaming & Other Essays* (Melbourne: Black Inc. Agenda, 2009), 58.

(6-34) The tales are a kind of commentary, or statement, on what is thought to be permanent and ordained at the very basis of the world and life. They are a way of stating the principle which animates things. I would call them a poetic key to Reality.

'The Dreaming' (1953), in *The Dreaming & Other Essays* (Melbourne: Black Inc. Agenda, 2009), 61.

(6-35) …'a philosophy' in the garb of an oral literature.

'The Dreaming' (1953), in *The Dreaming & Other Essays* (Melbourne: Black Inc. Agenda, 2009), 62.

T.G.H. (TED) STREHLOW
On connection to country

(6-36) …the native does not regard the various physical objects in the landscape which figure in his myths as mere monumental mounts or signposts … they are the handiwork of ancestors from whom he himself has descended. He sees recorded in the surrounding landscape the ancient story of the lives and deeds of the immortal beings whom he reveres… The whole countryside is his living, age-old family tree.

Aranda Traditions (Melbourne: Melbourne University Press, 1947), 29-31.

DONALD F. THOMSON
On the prestige attached to trade items

(6-37) …they acquire a halo of glamour and romance by reason of the way they are acquired; because they have *marr*. … this gives those acquired by ceremonial exchange a history, a background, a personality which lifts them above other *wakkinngu* objects and gives them a greatly enhanced value in the eyes of the people who receive them. … Here then, is the nucleus of a great system of exchange…

Economic structure and the ceremonial exchange cycle in Arnhem Land (Melbourne: Macmillan, 1949), 80.

ROBERT TONKINSON
On the dialectic between aggregation and dispersal

(6-38) The mode of adaptation of the Mardudjara involves a continuing dialectic between the ecological constraints that push people apart and the cultural pressures that draw them together.

The Mardudjara Aborigines: Living the dream in Australia's Desert (New York: Holt, Rinehart & Winston, 1978), 30.

On a conservative ideology

(6-39) …nowhere does their ideology admit structural change as a possibility.

The Mardudjara Aborigines: Living the dream in Australia's Desert (New York: Holt, Rinehart & Winston, 1978), 112.

WILLIAM JOHN WILLS
On nardoo as a poor but filling food

(6-40) ...I can only look out, like Mr. Micawber, for 'something
to turn up'; starvation on nardoo is by no means very
unpleasant...

A successful exploration through the interior of Australia (London: Richard
Bentley, 1863), 302.

JAMES WOODBURN
On the hunter-gatherer economy

(6-41) Australians [are] farmers in disguise who are concerned
with farming (and farming out) their women.

'Hunters and gatherers today and reconstruction of the past', in
E. Gellner (ed.), *Soviet and Western Anthropology* (London: Duckworth,
1980), 95-117, 108-9.

7: ON THE ROLE OF FIRE

The Australian continent has been dramatically shaped by fire and fire-makers. These quotations reflect on fire as a cultural artefact and the impact on landscapes, society and biota.

GEOFFREY BLAINEY
On the symbolic potential of the firestick

(7-1) If the hundreds of small independent aboriginal societies which once occupied Australia adopted a coat of arms, an appropriate emblem would be a firestick. It was a symbol of their technology, often a sign of their achievement, and a refutation of any suggestion that they were prisoners of their land.

The Triumph of the Nomads: a history of ancient Australia (Melbourne: Sun Books, 1983), 83.

REBECCA BLIEGE BIRD ET AL.
On Aboriginal people as an ecological agent

(7-2) Aboriginal foragers ... thus construct their own ecosystem. Over time, small-game hunting creates a very different landscape than that under a natural or lightening regime: it rearranges habitat into smaller patches, creating more diversity at spatial scales equivalent to a human foraging range. ... Martu burning does not increase the absolute amount of fire, it rescales its temporal and spatial impact.

R. Bliege Bird, D.W. Bird, B.F. Codding, C.H. Parker and J.H. Jones, 'The "fire stick farming" hypothesis: Australian Aboriginal foraging strategies, biodiversity, and anthropogenic fire mosaics', *Proceedings of the National Academy of Sciences* 105(39) (2008), 14796-14801, 14799-14800.

JAMES COOK
An initial reflection on the Australian coastline

(7-3) …this continent of smoke…

The Journals of Captain James Cook (Cambridge: Cambridge University Press, 1968), 263.

EDWARD CURR
On Aboriginal use of fire

(7-4) There was another instrument in the hands of these savages, which must be credited with results which it would be difficult to overestimate. I refer to the fire-stick; for the blackfellow was constantly setting fire to the grass and trees, both accidentally, and systematically for hunting purposes. Living principally on wild roots and animals, he tilled his land and cultivated his pastures with fire; and we shall not, perhaps, be far from the truth if we conclude that almost every part of New Holland was swept over by a fierce fire, on an average, once in every five years. That such constant and extensive conflagrations could have occurred without something more than temporary consequences seems impossible…

Recollections of Squatting in Victoria (Melbourne: G. Robertson, 1883), 88.

(7-5) …it may perhaps be doubted whether any section of the human race has exercised a greater influence on the physical condition of any large portion of the globe than the wandering savages of Australia.

Recollections of Squatting in Victoria (Melbourne: G. Robertson, 1883), 189-190.

CHARLES DARWIN
On the prevalence of fire

(7-6) In the whole country I scarcely saw a place without the

marks of a fire; whether these had been more or less recent –
whether the stumps were more or less black, was the greatest
change which varied the uniformity, so wearisome to the
traveller's eye.

Journal of Researches: Voyage of the Beagle (London: John Murray, 1845), 441.

H.H. (HEDLEY) FINLAYSON
On hunting fires

(7-7) …matters are so arranged that the areas where maala tracks
are thickest are within the lines of flame, and upon this space
attention is focused … The world seems full of flame and
smoke … they swing their weight from foot to foot, twirling
their throwing-sticks in their palms, and as they scan the
advancing flames their great eyes glow and sparkle as the
climax of the day draws near. It is their sport, their spectacle,
and their meat getting, all in one; and in it they taste a simple
intensity of joy which is beyond the range of our feeling.

The red centre: man and beast in the heart of Australia (Sydney: Angus &
Robertson, 1935), 63.

BILL GAMMAGE
On Aboriginal land management and a definition of 'estate'

(7-8) *estate*: Australia including Tasmania. Although comprising
many ways of maintaining land, and managers mostly
unknown to each other, this vast area was governed by a
single religious philosophy, called in English the Dreaming.

The Biggest Estate on Earth: How Aborigines Made Australia (Sydney: Allen
& Unwin, 2011), xix.

ERNEST GILES
On Aboriginal fires in central Australia

(7-9) …the natives were about, burning, burning, ever burning; one

would think they were of the fabled salamander race, and
lived on fire instead of water.

Australia Twice Traversed, vol. 1 (London: S. Low, Marston, Searle &
Rivington, Limited, 1889), 81.

TOM GRIFFITHS
On fire as a cultural artefact

(7-10) The history of fire, like the history of wilderness, slips
continually between the realms of the natural and the
cultural, from the study of an independent phenomenon to
the analysis of an artefact.

'History and natural history: Conservation movements in conflict?',
Australian Historical Studies 24(96) (1991), 16-32, 24.

SYLVIA HALLAM
On the effects of Aboriginal burning

(7-11) The land the English settled was not as God made it. It was
as the Aborigines made it.

*Fire and hearth: a study of Aboriginal usage and European usurpation in
south-western Australia* (Canberra: Australian Institute of Aboriginal
Studies, 1975), vii.

On the ancient and changing role of fire on the Swan River

(7-12) …although Aborigines had used fire throughout their
tenure of the continent, it is only from the times of final
rise of sea level that the evidence of caves, dunes and
swamps shows humanly initiated fire beginning to make
any real impact on the South-west coastal plain. … Fire
usage culminated in the last two millennia in the systematic
regulation, the 'burning by consecutive portions', found
throughout the South-west at contact.

*Fire and hearth: a study of Aboriginal usage and European usurpation in
south-western Australia* (Canberra: Australian Institute of Aboriginal
Studies, 1975), 112.

DAVID HORTON
On the impact of fire on the giant marsupials

(7-13) If creating grasslands in Australia was good for cows and
sheep, such effects would have been just as good for the
Diprotodons.

*The Pure State of Nature: Sacred Cows, Destructive Myths and the
Environment* (St Leonards, NSW: Allen & Unwin, 2000), 119.

RHYS JONES
On firestick farming

(7-14) Fire was man's first 'extra-corporeal muscle'.

'Fire-stick Farming', *Australian Natural History* 16 (1969), 224-228, 228.

(7-15) At the most general level, firing of the bush, in the same
way as clearing a forest to create a field, increased the
proportion of solar energy per unit area of the ground
that man could utilize. Perhaps we should call what the
Aborigines did 'fire-stick farming'.

'Fire-stick Farming', *Australian Natural History* 16 (1969), 224-228, 227.

A prehistorian's view of fire management

(7-16) Do we want to conserve the environment as it was in 1788,
or do we yearn for an environment without man, as it might
have been 30,000 or more years ago?

'Fire-stick Farming', *Australian Natural History* 16 (1969), 224-228, 228.

PETER KERSHAW
Fire as a consequence of climatic transitions

(7-17) Any change in vegetation, regardless of whether it was
in response to a wetter or drier climate, was likely to be
accompanied by an increase in burning... Vegetation

changes are facilitated by fire once climate change has
placed existing vegetation under stress.

'An Extended Late Quaternary Vegetation Record from North-Eastern
Queensland and its Implications for the Seasonal Tropics of Australia',
Proceedings of the Ecological Society of Australia 13 (1985), 179-189, 187.

LUDWIG LEICHHARDT
On systematic burning regimes

(7-18) The natives seemed to have burned the grass systematically
along every watercourse, and around every water-hole, in
order to have them surrounded with young grass as soon as
the rain sets in… It is no doubt connected with a systematic
management of their runs to attract game to particular
spots in the same way that stockholders burn parts of theirs.

*Journal of an overland expedition in Australia from Moreton Bay to Port
Essington: a distance of upwards of 3000 miles, during the years, 1844-1845*
(London: Boone, 1847), 354.

DUNCAN MERRILEES
On the role of fire in the extinction of megafauna

(7-19) If man arrived in Australia with 'peripatetic pyromania' as
part of his cultural tradition, his arrival may be marked in
archaeological deposits by sudden increase in abundance
of charcoal. If his arrival was followed by rapid decline to
extinction of many marsupial species, especially of the larger,
more easily hunted kinds, this may be revealed directly in
archaeological deposits or marked by a trend away from
skinning knives, scrapers and other devices for dealing with
large game animals towards millstones or other devices for
dealing with plant food and small game, or even possibly by
decline in human population.

'Man the destroyer: late Quaternary changes in the Australian marsupial
fauna', *Journal of the Royal Society of Western Australia* 51 (1968), 1-24, 20.

THOMAS MITCHELL
On the interdependence of game and fire

(7-20) Fire, grass, kangaroos, and human inhabitants, seem all
dependent on each other for existence in Australia; for any
one of these being wanting, the others could no longer
continue.

*Journal of an expedition into the interior of tropical Australia, in search of a
route from Sydney to the Gulf of Carpentaria* (London: Longman, Brown,
Green and Longmans, 1848), 249.

BILL NEIDJIE
A Gagudju perspective on fire

(7-21) This earth...
I never damage
I look after.
Fire is nothing,
just clean up.
...
I don't know about white European way,
We, Aborigine, burn...
Make things grow.

B. Neidjie, S. Davis and A. Fox, *Kakadu man...Bill Neidjie* (Darwin:
Mybrood, 1986), 35.

MARK O'CONNOR
On fire-stick farming

(7-22) In the hot calm the bees are loud,
working wings and elbows with an angry sound,
as you leap the tussocks, amazed
at your ignorant creation,
the shapes and passions hidden
in a sheet of flame.

And above them all
a new forest rising.

'Fire-stick Farming', in *Fire-stick Farming: Selected Poems 1972-90*
(Sydney: Hale & Iremonger, 1990), 132.

STEPHEN J. PYNE
On the Australian Pyrophile

(7-23) In the Aborigine, Australian fire had discovered an
extraordinary ally. Not only did ignition sources multiply
and spread, but fire itself persisted through wet season and
dry, across grassland and forest, in desert and on mountain.
Lightning was a highly seasonal, episodic ignition source;
the Aboriginal firestick was an eternal flame.

Burning bush: a fire history of Australia (New York: Henry Holt and
Company, 1991), 91.

On the fire continent

(7-24) Australia is, more than any other, a fire continent, and
because of that fact it shows with special clarity the power
and limitations of the pact humanity has with fire. … The
other continents fire touched; Australia, it branded. Fires
dapple Australian geography and punctuate Australian
history.

World Fire: The Culture of Fire on Earth (New York: Holt, 1995), 29.

GEORGE SEDDON
On the 'man-modified environment' of Australia

(7-25) …the most important fact in the environmental history of
Australia is that it had a radically new technology imposed
on it, suddenly, twice.

'The Man-Modified Environment', in J. McLaren (ed.), *A Nation Apart*
(Melbourne: Longman Cheshire, 1983), 9-31, 10.

MIKE SMITH
On people as another source of ignition

(7-26) Bit by bit, people have been reduced to just another source of ignition, with climate setting the parameters of any impact.

'Palaeoclimates: An archaeology of climate change', in T. Sherrat, T. Griffiths and L. Robin (eds.), *A change in the weather: climate & culture in Australia* (Canberra: National Museum of Australia Press, 2005), 176-186, 185.

CHARLES STURT
On the Australian landscape as a gentleman's park

(7-27) In many places the trees are so sparingly, and I had almost said judiciously distributed as to resemble the park lands attached to a gentleman's residence in England, and it only wants the edifice to complete the comparison.

Narrative of an expedition into Central Australia, performed under the authority of Her Majesty's government during the years 1844, 5, and 6: together with a notice of the province of South Australia in 1847, vol. 2 (London: T. and W. Boone, 1849), 230.

NORMAN B. TINDALE
On Aboriginal modification of the environment

(7-28) …man has had such a profound effect on the distributions of forest and grassland that true primaeval forest may be far less common in Australia than is generally realised, as indeed it is relatively rare in all lands where man has intruded for lengthy periods of time.

'Ecology of primitive man in Australia', in A.L. Keast, R.L. Crocker & C.S. Christian (eds.), *Biogeography and Ecology in Australia* (The Hague: W. Junk, 1959), 36-51, 43.

8: ON THE POLITICS OF PREHISTORY

In a settler society on Aboriginal land, archaeology is inevitably seen as a political activity, and, as these quotations show, its narratives have now entered the public life of the nation.

TONY ABBOTT
On Australian prehistory

(8-1) We have to acknowledge that pre-1788 this land was as Aboriginal then as it is Australian now and until we have acknowledged that, we will be an incomplete nation and a torn people. ...our challenge is to do now in these times what should have been done 200 or 100 years ago: to acknowledge Aboriginal people in our foundation document.

Opposition Leader Tony Abbott, Second Reading Speech, Aboriginal and Torres Strait Islander Peoples Recognition Bill, House of Representatives, 13 February 2013.

On the prehistory of Botany Bay

(8-2) As we look around this glorious city, as we see the extraordinary development, it's hard to think that back in 1788 it was nothing but bush and that the marines, and the convicts and the sailors that struggled off those 12 ships just a few hundred yards from where we are now, must have thought they'd come almost to the moon.

Prime Minister Tony Abbott, quoted in A. Henderson, 'Prime Minister Tony Abbott describes Sydney as "nothing but bush" before First Fleet arrived in 1788', ABC News, 14 November 2014.

HARRY ALLEN
On the preservation of Aboriginal sites

(8-3) Australians feel they are cut off from the heritage of their past homelands and from the heritage of their new homelands as well. Historians and archaeologists, through the 'Heritage Movement', have become involved in their own attempt to establish spiritual and emotional ties between Europeans and the land by taking over control of the material links that existed between Aborigines, the land, and its past in the form of archaeological and sacred sites. These are not being preserved because of their value to Aboriginal society but for their value to the Europeans.

'History Matters: a commentary on divergent interpretations of Australian history', *Australian Aboriginal Studies* 2 (1988), 79-89, 86.

On archaeology's political role

(8-4) Archaeologists must lose some of their power and drop their vested interests in keeping control of the discipline and the country's historical resources and actively foster Aboriginal involvement on an equal basis. The first task is to acknowledge that our studies play an important role in contemporary Australian society and to begin the debate on what exactly that role might be.

'History Matters: a commentary on divergent interpretations of Australian history', *Australian Aboriginal Studies* 2 (1988), 79-89, 88.

ROBYNE BANCROFT
On archaeological fieldwork by Isabel McBryde

(8-5) These are very important sites for my people: it was your research that has assisted in the recognition of [their] archaeological importance complementing our oral traditions.

'Isabel McBryde: mentor, groundbreaker, teacher and friend', in I. Macfarlane, M.J. Mountain and R. Paton (eds.), *Many Exchanges: archaeology, history, community and the work of Isabel McBryde* (Canberra: Aboriginal History Inc., 2005), 47-48, 47.

JIM BOWLER
On the discoveries at Lake Mungo

(8-6) This not only changed the dimension of Australian history but, in a special sense, it also changed the whole notion of being Australian. The realisation that this land nourished and was known by whole populations of people for 40,000 years instantly changed the nature of that landscape.

'Reading the Australian landscape: European and Aboriginal perspectives', *Cappuccino papers* 1 (Melbourne: Imagine The Future Inc, 1995).

(8-7) In my pursuit of rational science, those lakeshore sands, originally solely of geological interest, have been transformed into sacred grounds. My eyes have been opened to glimpse and share in some small way that inner view long entrusted to Mungo Man's Aboriginal descendants, a deep connection to country, to their ancestral spirit-charged lands. I remain ever conscious of Mutthi Mutthi elder Mary Pappin's admonition: 'You did not find Mungo Lady and Mungo Man – they found you!'

'Mungo Man is a physical reminder of the need for Indigenous recognition', *Guardian Australia*, 25 February 2014.

(8-8) …the realisation that the Australian landscape has been humanised for tens of thousands of years has yet to be welded into the Australian conscience.

'Reading the Australian landscape: European and Aboriginal perspectives', *Cappuccino papers* 1 (Melbourne: Imagine The Future Inc, 1995).

DENIS BYRNE
On appropriation of an indigenous past

(8-9) Yet surely, on the face of it, there is something quite radical and extraordinary in the prospect of a settler culture which for so long had pronounced indigenous culture to be a savage anachronism suddenly turning to embrace the past of that culture as its own.

'Deep nation: Australia's acquisition of an indigenous past', *Aboriginal History* 20 (1998), 82-107, 82.

GRAHAME CLARK
On the importance of a common, global past

(8-10) To peoples of the world generally, the peoples who willy nilly must in future co-operate and build or fall out and destroy, I venture to suggest that Palaeolithic Man has more meaning than the Greeks.

'Education and the Study of Man' (1943), in *Economic Prehistory* (Cambridge: Cambridge University Publishing, 1989), 410.

KIRSTY DOUGLAS
On a new aesthetic at Lake Mungo

(8-11) The deep past provides a new aesthetic, according to which the sparse, worn, dry, goat-infested landscape is reconfigured as an 'eerie, yet beautiful, moonscape', 'a constant source of mystery and delight', spectacular, surreal and dramatic. Tourist destination, World Heritage region, geomorphological text book, archaeological wonderland, National Park, Aboriginal sacred site, contested country: the lakes landscapes, especially the Walls of China lunette, are now unambiguously national landscapes.

Pictures of time beneath: science, heritage and the uses of the deep past (Collingwood, VIC: CSIRO Publishing, 2010), 148.

On the symbolism of Mungo

(8-12) Material remains of the past are cultural artefacts with
powerful political resonance. They are part of the fabric
for the construction of an illusory national unity, the glue
which sticks us to the land. ... The Mungo remains are
reconfigured as Adam and Eve, symbolising the professional
beginnings of a discipline and the backward extension of
a nation as much as the spiritual heart of an Indigenous
population and perhaps a new beginning for academic-
Aboriginal reconciliation.

Pictures of time beneath: science, heritage and the uses of the deep past
(Collingwood, VIC: CSIRO Publishing, 2010), 156.

ROBERT EDWARDS
On the importance of conservation and cultural tourism

(8-13) Aboriginal monuments pose a problem of a different order
as they are not fully accepted as part of Australian history...
The great prehistoric monuments, ancient buildings, rich
cave art and other relics of Europe are the product of the
predecessors of existing populations. National pride ensures
their preservation: cultural tourism provides an added
incentive. So far there is no comparable attitude towards
Aboriginal antiquities in Australia and their conservation
has been relegated to low priority... Future generations
will not forgive us if we allow the destruction of our rich
cultural heritage.

'Tourism in Australia and Overseas', in R. Edwards (ed.), *The Preservation
of Australia's Aboriginal Heritage* (Canberra: Australian Institute of
Aboriginal Studies, 1975), 37-47, 37.

On the international significance of Arnhem Land art

(8-14) ...the Obiri paintings are some of the best examples of
Aboriginal art in Arnhem Land and among the best in

Australia. In international terms, they rate with the great Palaeolithic art sites of France and Spain and the Bushmen paintings of Africa.

Australian Aboriginal Art: The art of the Alligator Rivers region, Northern Territory (Canberra: Australian Institute of Aboriginal Studies, 1979), 69.

PETER GATHERCOLE
On history for everybody

(8-15) It is said that when Jack Golson, an archaeologist at the Australian National University, advertised a lecture in Port Moresby entitled '50 000 years of Papua New Guinea history' (the evidence for which was mainly archaeological), people trekked for miles to hear him. Hitherto, history had been about white people. Now it would be about everybody.

'Introduction', in P. Gathercole and D. Lowenthal, *The politics of the past* (London: Routledge, 1994), 1-6, 1.

PEARL GIBBS
On Indigenous heritage

(8-16) There's no white men, or woman, who has that feeling we have. They can study us all they like, but we've got them studied too. Because this is *our* country… It belongs to us, it is precious to us. And that is something no white man will ever understand…

Quoted in K. Gilbert, *Because A White Man'll Never Do It* (Sydney: Angus and Robertson, 1973), 12-13.

SYLVIA HALLAM
On dispossession of the land

(8-17) The European communities inherited the possibilities of settlement and land-use from the Aboriginal communities.

But in doing so, they robbed these communities of the land which had mapped out the patterns of their existence.

Fire and hearth: a study of Aboriginal usage and European usurpation in south-western Australia (Canberra: Australian Institute of Aboriginal Studies, 1975), 65.

On women and archaeological practice

(8-18) Are only women sufficiently tough, conscientious and foolhardy to collect and analyse such a mass of trivia, and hammer it into meaning and shape?

'Review: The Moth Hunters: Aboriginal Prehistory of the Australian Alps', *Aboriginal History* 6 (1982), 154-159, 154.

PETER HISCOCK
On a dynamic prehistory

(8-19) ...the history of humanity in this continent has been dynamic and evolving, and we must appreciate it as such. We should not hide this remarkable record of adaptation and evolution behind slogans such as 'Aboriginal culture is the longest continuing culture in the world', a slogan that implies a lack of cultural change, a Western myth of an ethnographic present stretching back fifty thousand years.

'Creators or Destroyers? The Burning Questions of Human Impact in Ancient Aboriginal Australia', *Humanities Australia* 5 (2014), 40-52, 45.

On celebrating change in the archaeological record

(8-20) Archaeological research encourages us to celebrate change and adaptability of human life in ancient Australia, not to demand that the past be merely the same as the present world; a view that pretends Aboriginal culture (or indeed all culture) has changed little. The dynamic reality of the human past, revealed everywhere in archaeological research, is far more interesting and challenging.

Concluding words, *The Archaeology of Ancient Australia* (London: Routledge, 2008), 285.

DAVID HORTON
On managing the environment

(8-21) If we need a model for caring for the Australian environment, then it is not a time for outsourcing to Europe or America. We have a home-grown job applicant with 50,000 years of experience.

The Pure State of Nature: Sacred Cows, Destructive Myths and the Environment (St Leonards, NSW: Allen & Unwin, 2000), 168.

PETER HOWSON
The Minister for the Environment, Aborigines and the Arts on Aboriginal antiquities

(8-22) The evidence of man's ancient occupation of Australia is, in an important sense, part of the heritage of all men everywhere.

Howson, 1972, quoted in R. Edwards (ed.), *The Preservation of Australia's Aboriginal Heritage* (Canberra: Australian Institute of Aboriginal Studies, 1975), 3.

PAUL KEATING
On coming to terms with the Aboriginal past

(8-23) We are beginning to learn what the indigenous people have known for many thousands of years – how to live with our physical environment. Ever so gradually we are learning how to see Australia through Aboriginal eyes, beginning to recognise the wisdom contained in their epic story. … We cannot imagine that the descendants of people whose genius and resilience maintained a culture

here through fifty thousand years or more, through
cataclysmic changes to the climate and environment, and
who then survived two centuries of dispossession and
abuse, will be denied their place in the modern Australian
nation. We cannot imagine that.

Prime Minister Paul Keating, Redfern Speech (Year for the World's
Indigenous People), Delivered in Redfern Park, 10 December 1992.

ALICE KELLY
On the return of the Mungo I and III burials

(8-24) We want her to be put right back where she came from ... I
want him brought back and put down in the same place.

A. Kelly, Mutthi Mutthi elder, quoted in S. Colley, *Uncovering
Australia: archaeology, indigenous people and the public* (Washington, DC:
Smithsonian Institution Press, 2002), 165.

ROSALIND LANGFORD
On Indigenous control of archaeological heritage

(8-25) The issue is control. You seek to say that as scientists
you have a right to obtain and study information of our
culture. You seek to say that because you are Australians
you have a right to study and explore our heritage because
it is a heritage to be shared by all Australians, white and
black. From our point of view, we say – you have come
as invaders, you have tried to destroy our culture, you
have built your fortunes upon the lands and bodies of our
people, and now, having said sorry, want a share in picking
out the bones of what you regard as a dead past. We say
that it is our past, our culture and heritage, and forms part
of our present life. As such it is ours to control and it is
ours to share on our terms.

'Our heritage – Your playground', *Australian Archaeology* 16 (1983), 1-6, 2.

(8-26) ...if we Aborigines cannot control our own heritage, *what the hell can we control?* It seems that whites, whether they be pastoralists, philosophers or archaeologists, not only deny our right to our land but now want to deny us the right to our heritage.

'Our heritage – Your playground', *Australian Archaeology* 16 (1983), 1-6, 4.

MARCIA LANGTON
On the Australian Institute of Aboriginal and Torres Strait Islander Studies

(8-27) There cannot be any doubt that teaching and research about Aboriginal society adds dignity to humankind as a whole. It is an essential means of leading other Australians to greater tolerance and understanding.

'A Fireside Chat', in T. Bonyhady and T. Griffiths (eds.), *Prehistory to Politics: John Mulvaney, the Humanities and the Public Intellectual* (Melbourne: Melbourne University Press, 1996), 134-143, 142.

On Aboriginal land management

(8-28) I suggest that Aboriginal people and their land management traditions have also been rendered invisible in Australian landscapes, not only by legal but also by 'science fictions' that arise from the assumption of superiority of Western knowledge over indigenous knowledge systems, the result of which is, often, a failure to recognise the critical relevance of these latter to sustainable environmental management.

Burning questions: emerging environmental issues for indigenous peoples in Northern Australia (Darwin: Northern Territory University, 1998), 9.

On colonising culture

(8-29) Our culture is no longer simply a country for anthropologists, New Age mystics and wilderness campaigners to colonise. Their tragic, necrophiliac and self-serving accounts are no competition for the works of the new guard of Aboriginal creative workers, nor for actual Aboriginal culture.

The Quiet Revolution: Indigenous people and the resources boom, Boyer Lectures 2012 (Sydney: Harper Collins, 2013), 149.

DOROTHY LAWSON
A Mutthi Mutthi perspective on the Pleistocene cremation-burial at Lake Mungo

(8-30) She surfaced for a reason.

Comment in A. Pike and A. McGrath, *Message from Mungo*, Ronin films (2014).

BARRY LOPEZ
On destruction of sites

(8-31) The vandals, the few who crowbar rock art off the desert's walls, who dig up graves, who punish the ground that holds intaglios, are people who devour history. Their self-centered scorn, their disrespect for ideas and images beyond their ken, create the awful atmosphere of loose ends in which totalitarianism thrives, in which the past is merely curious or wrong.

Crossing Open Ground (New York: Scribner's, 1988), 16.

DAVID LOWENTHAL
On stretching history into the mists of prehistory

(8-32) To compensate for the absence of a long recorded history, we are prone to stretch history back into the mists of prehistory. The Australian heritage incorporates not only the few decades since the European discovery but the long reaches of unrecorded time comprised in Aboriginal life and, before that, in the history of nature itself, the animals and plants and the very rocks of the Australian continent. Thus the felt past expands, enabling Australia to equal the antiquity of any nation.

'Australian Images: The Unique Present, The Mythical Past', in P. Quartermaine (ed.), *Readings in Australian Arts: Papers from 1976* (Exeter: University of Exeter, 1978), 84-93, 86.

ISABEL MCBRYDE
On the appropriation of the past

(8-33) As archaeologists have we taken possession of a past that is not ours, and either unwittingly or paternally collaborated in its appropriation as symbol of national identity?

'Past and present indivisible? Archaeology and society, archaeology in society', in T. Bonyhady and T. Griffiths (eds.), *Prehistory to Politics: John Mulvaney, the Humanities and the Public Intellectual* (Melbourne: Melbourne University Press, 1996), 63-84, 74.

VINCENT MEGAW
On the archaeology in the public domain

(8-34) I have mentioned here the public, a dirty word to many who over the years have seen what only misinformed ignorance and a lack of historical awareness can do to the physical remains of the unique aspects of Australia's heritage.

'Australian Archaeology: how far have we progressed?', *Mankind* 6(7) (1966), 306-12, 308.

THOMAS MITCHELL
On the dispossession of a worked landscape

(8-35) How natural must be the aversion of the natives to the intrusion of another race of men with cattle: people who recognise no right in the aborigines to either the grass they

have thus worked from infancy, nor to the kangaroos they
have hunted with their fathers.

*Journal of an expedition into the interior of tropical Australia, in search of a
route from Sydney to the Gulf of Carpentaria* (London: Longman, Brown,
Green and Longmans, 1848), 306.

JOHN MULVANEY
On early settler attitudes towards Aboriginal people

(8-36) …many eminent Victorians treated Australia as a museum
of primeval humanity and a storehouse of fossil culture. In
the great dispute between apes and angels, the Aborigines
were ranged firmly on the side of the apes. The Aboriginal
became the type of primitive man.

'The Australian Aborigines 1606-1929: Opinion and Fieldwork',
Australian Historical Studies 8 (1958), 131-51, 297-314, 297.

On the role of prehistorians

(8-37) Prehistorians are in a position to emphasise the dignity
and individuality of the society which colonised the sixth
continent, to document its diversity through time and
across regions, and to preserve its monuments through time.

'Blood from Stones and Bones: Aboriginal Australians and Australian
Prehistory', *Search* 10(6) (1979), 214-18, 218.

On the modern reburial of ancient skeletal remains

(8-38) …a triumph of bureaucracy and irrationality over prudence
and positive, collaborative racial relations… Past repressive
colonialism does not mean that the present academic
generation must pay the price, by never opposing strident
claims and demands by radical Aboriginal leaders. Not to
do so, will be to replace white violence and repression with
black intellectual totalitarianism. It is not simply the Kow
Swamp relics which are at stake, but the future of past

Aboriginal culture, and the freedom of all peoples of any
race to study it.

'Past regained, future lost: The Kow Swamp Pleistocene burials', *Antiquity*
65(246) (1991), 12-13.

KEN MULVANEY
On development in the Dampier Archipelago

(8-39) Today the Dampier Archipelago contains arguably the
world's foremost collection of petroglyphs whilst also
contending for the world's largest bulk export port. ... Until
the area's cultural and natural values are placed higher than
its industrialisation, there seems little that will sway the
continued transformation of this rugged and beautiful
landscape, which cradles the cultural achievements of
people throughout many tens of millennia, with the iconic
structures of an industrial nation. This archipelago contains
an irreplaceable cultural record that is tied to the location.
The rock art cannot move; it is future industry that can and
must be moved to alternate places.

'Dampier Archipelago: decades of development and destruction', *Rock art
research* 28(1) (2011), 17-25, 17, 23-24.

LES MURRAY AND JOHN HOWARD
Proposed wording for a constitutional preamble, 1999

(8-40) Since time immemorial our land has been inhabited by
Aborigines and Torres Strait Islanders, who are honoured
for their ancient and continuing cultures.

L. Murray and Prime Minister John Howard, quoted in M. McKenna,
'First Words: A Brief History of Public Debate on a New Preamble to the
Australian Constitution 1991-99', Parliamentary Library Research Paper
16 (1999-2000).

GEORGE ORWELL
On controlling the past

(8-41) Who controls the past controls the future: who controls the present controls the past.

Nineteen Eighty-Four (New York: Buccaneer Books, 1949), 251.

COLIN PARDOE
On prehistory

(8-42) Aboriginal and Torres Strait Islander history is the history of Australia, and as such can not be segregated or relegated to the outskirts of Australian society or to 'prehistory'.

'Sharing the past: Aboriginal influence on archaeological practice, a case study from New South Wales', *Aboriginal History* 14 (1990), 208-223, 208.

NOEL PEARSON
An indigenous perspective on modern Australia

(8-43) Our nation is in three parts. There is our ancient heritage, written in the continent and the original culture painted on its land and seascapes. There is its British inheritance, the structures of government and society transported from the United Kingdom fixing its foundations in the ancient soil. There is its multicultural achievement: a triumph of immigration that brought together the gifts of peoples and cultures from all over the globe – forming one indissoluble commonwealth.

A rightful place: race, recognition and a more complete commonwealth, Quarterly Essay 55 (Collingwood, VIC: Black Inc. Books, 2014), 55.

On the classical culture of ancient Australia

(8-44) ...the songlines of the women of central Australia are also the heritage of non-Aboriginal Australians. It is this culture that is the Iliad and Odyssey of Australia. It is these mythic stories that are Australia's Book of Genesis. For the shards of classical culture of this continent to vanish would be a loss not only to its indigenous peoples but also to all Australians, and to the heritage of the world generally. We would be poorer for the loss.

A rightful place: race, recognition and a more complete commonwealth, Quarterly Essay 55 (Collingwood, VIC: Black Inc. Books, 2014), 36.

On the value of early research

(8-45) It is no exaggeration to say that the notebooks and journals of the researchers who worked in Cape York Peninsular these past fifty years are themselves part of the world's heritage.

A rightful place: race, recognition and a more complete commonwealth, Quarterly Essay 55 (Collingwood, VIC: Black Inc. Books, 2014), 70.

CHARLES PERKINS
On an ancient culture

(8-46) Our culture goes back 70,000 years and is easily identifiable. We must build on our great strength – the spirit and dignity of our people.

A Bastard Like Me (Sydney: Ure Smith, 1975), 189-190.

COLIN RENFREW AND PAUL BAHN
On the politics of the past

(8-47) The past is big business – in tourism and in the auction rooms. The past is politically highly charged, ideologically powerful and significant. And the past, or what remains of it, is subject to increasing destruction.

Archaeology: Theories, Methods, and Practice (London: Thames and Hudson, 1991), 463.

KEVIN RUDD
Apology to the Stolen Generations

(8-48) I move: That today we honour the Indigenous peoples of
this land, the oldest continuing cultures in human history.
We reflect on their past mistreatment. ... We embrace with
pride, admiration and awe these great and ancient cultures
we are truly blessed to have among us – cultures that
provide a unique, uninterrupted human thread linking our
Australian continent to the most ancient prehistory of our
planet.

Prime Minister Kevin Rudd, 'Apology to Australia's Indigenous peoples',
Parliament of Australia, House of Representatives, 13 February 2008.

CARMEL SCHRIRE
On archaeological empathy

(8-49) In recent years, the consequences of repatriation and
cultural restitution have given the impression that only the
dispossessed can lay claim to pain, and only the indigene to
a soul. The ensuing polarization of archaeologists and native
peoples sometimes makes one forget it was not always so:
archaeologists have not always been cast as strangers, and
their research has often been motivated by a deep affinity
and empathy for the people they uncover.

'Betrayal as a universal element in the sundering of Bass Strait', in A.
Anderson, I. Lilley and S. O'Connor (eds.), *Histories of Old Ages: Essays in
Honour of Rhys Jones* (Canberra: Pandanus Books, 2001), 25-33, 25.

BERNARD SMITH
On historical inquiry in Australia

(8-50) White Australians have tried to forget. Indeed at times it
would seem as if all the culture of old Europe were being
brought to bear upon our writers and artists in order to

blot from their memories the crimes perpetrated upon Australia's first inhabitants. In recent years however both sides, black and white alike, have become aware increasingly of the continuing colonial crime, the locked cupboard of our history.

The Spectre of Truganini: The 1980 Boyer Lectures (Sydney: ABC, 1980), 18.

MIKE SMITH
On the rationale for modern archaeological research

(8-51) Baldwin Spencer presented Aboriginal society as a relict of an early stage in social evolution. Modern archaeological research in Australia, New Guinea and the Pacific region began as a reaction to this view, taking the position that the peoples of the region had their own histories which could be recovered using archaeological field techniques.

'Central Australia and the 1894 Horn Expedition', in S.R. Morton and D.J. Mulvaney (eds.), *Exploring Central Australia: Society, the Environment and the 1894 Horn Expedition* (Chipping Norton, NSW: Surrey Beatty & Sons, 1996), 60-73, 71.

On archaeology as a gift

(8-52) There is a history here. It is something that sits next to the Dreaming. It doesn't displace it, it doesn't replace it, but it's a rich history here, it's something to be proud of... It's been my privilege to work on this history, but in a sense it has also been my gift.

'Mike Smith interviewed by Tom Griffiths', National Library of Australia, 8 June 2012.

On the destruction of a totemic landscape by iron ore mining

(8-53) It's not just that people are losing control over the sites or losing access to lands, the actual land is being shipped off to China. I mean… there goes the Dreaming! There goes the body of the ancestral beings!

'Mike Smith interviewed by Tom Griffiths', National Library of Australia, 8 June 2012.

W.E.H. (BILL) STANNER
On the 'great Australian silence'

(8-54) It is a structural matter, a view from a window which has been carefully placed to exclude a whole quadrant of the landscape. What may well have begun as a simple forgetting of other possible views turned under habit and over time into something like a cult of forgetfulness practised on a national scale. We have been able for so long to disremember the aborigines that we are now hard put to keep them in mind even when we most want to do so.

After the dreaming: black and white Australians, Boyer Lectures, 1968 (Sydney: ABC, 1969), 25.

SHARON SULLIVAN
On controlling access to sites

(8-55) …whoever controls research into such sites controls, to some extent, the Aboriginal past.

'The custodianship of Aboriginal sites in southeastern Australia', in Isabel McBryde (ed.), *Who Owns The Past* (Melbourne: Oxford University Press, 1985), 139-56, 139.

On heritage practices

(8-56) The way we practice heritage conservation in the west comes out of what I would call the Western Dreaming. By

this I mean the cultural assumptions that we take as given –
our own unconscious vision of our society and ourselves.

'Out of the box: Isabel McBryde's radical contribution to the shaping of
Australian archaeological practice', in I. Macfarlane, M.J. Mountain and
R. Paton (eds.), *Many Exchanges: archaeology, history, community and the
work of Isabel McBryde* (Canberra: Aboriginal History Inc., 2005), 83-94,
83.

On 'cowboy archaeology' as an exercise in machismo

(8-57) 'My Pleistocene sequence is bigger than your Pleistocene
sequence.'

Comment in A. Pike and A. McGrath, *Message from Mungo*, Ronin films
(2014).

PETER UCKO
On the politics of archaeology

(8-58) Aborigines are forcing archaeologists to recognize that
their discipline is one which sometimes can and does have
(extreme) political and social consequences.

'Australian academic archaeology: Aboriginal transformation of its aims
and practices', *Australian Archaeology* 16 (1983), 11-26, 20.

GOUGH WHITLAM
On Aboriginal Australia

(8-59) Let us never forget this: Australia's real test as far as the rest
of the world, and particularly our region, is concerned is the
role we create for our own Aborigines. In this sense, and it
is a very real sense, the Aborigines are our true link with our
region.

Opposition Leader Gough Whitlam, Election Policy Speech, delivered at
the Blacktown Civic Centre, Sydney, 13 November 1972.

INDEX BY AUTHOR

INDEX BY KEY PHRASE

NUMERALS

A

B

C

changed the whole notion of being Australian   BOWL 8-6
Changes in the numbers   HEAD 3-21
charting the oscillations of an unstable system   SMIT 3-40
Civilization exists by geological consent   DURA 4-10
Climate is an ill-tempered beast   BROE 4-3
clink of spade on hearth   HORT 3-23
clocks with no hands for ever drumming   THOM 3-45
Cloncurry axe, a Boulia boomerang   MULV 6-24
coastal way of life   BOWD 1-12
coat of arms   BLAI 7-1
complementing our oral traditions   BANC 8-5
considerable length of time   HOWC 1-41
constant if somewhat straggling trickle   BIRD 1-8
construct their own ecosystem   BLEI 7-2
continent of smoke   COOK 7-3
continent on survival rations   HORT 4-13
cool and awesome Gothic atmosphere   WRIG 1-93
cornerstone of prehistory is stratigraphy   MULV 2-68
count the pebbles   DARW 2-20
creativity of the human spirit   MULV 6-22
creatures, often crude and quaint   SPEN 6-32
creeping sterility in Australian archaeology   BOWD 2-10
crude and colourless ... industry   CLAR 1-21
cult of forgetfulness   STAN 8-54
cultural conservatism   GOUL 5-17
cultural history of the region as a whole   MCBR 2-61
curious relics for the family mantelpiece   MCBR 2-60
cut off from ... their past homelands   ALLE 8-3
cutting pieces out of a ... manuscript   BARK 2-4

D

dark continent of prehistory   MULV 1-64
Day by dreary day   MAYN 2-66
Dead archaeology is the driest dust that blows   WHEE 2-94

F

G

H

Hitherto, history had been about white people	GATH 8-15
holding country	MYER 6-25
home-grown job applicant	HORT 8-21
honeymoon is over	JONE 2-52
horribly boring unless you're a flint fan	CHIL 1-19
How much climate change	SMIT 4-33
hypercritical individuals	FLOO 2-31

I

I felt quite happy and perfectly indifferent	KING 6-17
I hankered after the Iron Age	MULV 2-71
I hate travelling and explorers	LEVI 2-58
I scarcely saw a place without … fire	DARW 7-6
I wanted to drive around in a big Landrover	SCHR 2-80
ideal labour force for the small excavation	ATKI 2-3
If women are archaeologically invisible	OCON 1-72
Iliad and Odyssey of Australia	PEAR 8-44
imagination has its own geography	GREE 3-18
immense periods of time	HOWI 1-42
immensity of the past	HEAD 3-20
'impact' should be reserved for meteorites	HEAD 1-35
imprint of past changes	BOWL 4-2
incomplete nation and a torn people	ABBO 8-1
ingenious team of lay botanists	FLAN 2-27
inherited the possibilities of settlement	HALL 8-17
inspiration of dreams	JONE 4-17
instant thick	WILM 3-47
intellectual dandyism	LEVI 6-18
interleaved and intercut elliptical hearths	JONE 1-49
international terms	EDWA 8-14
interplanetary archeologists of the future	LEE 3-30
inter-relationships *between* sites	KAMM 2-56
Is man a geological antiquity in Australia?	DAVI 3-8
islands of the interior	VETH 5-36

M

N

O

only the dispossessed	SCHR 8-49
orbital metronome	SMIT 3-40
original affluent society	SAHL 6-30
Our culture goes back 70,000 years	PERK 8-46
Our nation is in three parts	PEAR 8-43
Our story is in the land	NEID 6-26
our true link with our region	WHIT 8-59
ours to control and it is ours to share	LANG 8-25

P

Palaeolithic or Neolithic; Hunter or Farmer	JONE 4-16
Palaeolithic Man has more meaning	CLAR 8-10
paleoethnofemobotantists	BECK 2-7
palimpsest of different deserts	SMIT 4-31
Panaramitee style	ROSE 1-74
park lands … a gentleman's residence	STUR 7-27
part of the heritage of all men everywhere	HOWS 8-22
part of the world's heritage	PEAR 8-45
particular sensitivity	BOWL 4-2
past is big business	RENF 8-47
Perennial rivers drained into inland seas	MULV 1-65
'a philosophy' in the garb of an oral literature	STAN 6-35
Places die, just as men do	JOUB 4-20
Pleistocene ancestors … did things differently?	SHAW 2-82
poetic key to Reality	STAN 6-34
poor kind of fish	CHRI 2-13
poor world is almost six thousand years old	SHAK 3-39
poster-child for human antiquity	DOUG 4-9
prehistory as concerned with historical problems	MCBR 2-62
Prehistory down under	DORT 1-24
probably a beech, possibly an oak	TATE 4-36
public, a dirty word	MEGA 8-34
push people apart	TONK 6-38

Q

R

S

T

U

V

W

Y